T0271167

Tourism, Knowledge and Learning

This book contributes to the understanding of how tourism can be designed to provide conditions for learning. This involves learning for tourists, the tourist industry, public authorities and local communities. We explore how tourism, knowledge and learning can be used as means towards sustainable development through current, new or changed structures, concepts, activities and communication efforts. The book should be seen as both an inspiration for tourism actors (e.g. tourism attractions, policy makers and other industry actors), and a scholarly contribution to further research. A holistic approach distinguishes this book from most existing literature that focuses on separate units of tourism – for instance, personal or community well-being, nature-based tourism, cultural heritage tourism or tourism that is a result of researchers' travels (so-called scientific tourism). The various contributors to the book provide a range of perspectives and experiences, from social sciences with a focus on marketing, innovation management, human geography and environmental law, to arts and humanities with a focus on heritage studies, archaeology and photography and, finally, to natural sciences with a focus on marine sciences.

Eva Maria Jernsand is a researcher at the Department of Business Administration, University of Gothenburg, Sweden.

Maria Persson is a researcher at the Department of Historical Studies, University of Gothenburg, Sweden.

Erik Lundberg is a researcher and lecturer at the Department of Business Administration, University of Gothenburg, Sweden.

Routledge Insights in Tourism Series

This series provides a forum for cutting edge insights into the latest developments in tourism research. It offers high quality monographs and edited collections that develop tourism analysis at both theoretical and empirical levels.

Millennials, Spirituality and Tourism
Edited by Sandeep Kumar Walia and Aruditya Jasrotia

Tourism, Safety and COVID-19
Security, Digitization and Tourist Behaviour
Salvatore Monaco

COVID-19 and the Tourism Industry
Sustainability, Resilience and New Directions
Edited by Anukrati Sharma, Azizul Hassan and Priyakrushna Mohanty

Management of Tourism Ecosystem Services in a Post Pandemic Context
Global Perspectives
Edited by Vanessa Gaitree Gowreesunkar, Shem Wambugu Maingi and Felix L. M. Ming'ate

Tourism, Knowledge and Learning
Edited by Eva Maria Jernsand, Maria Persson and Erik Lundberg

For more information about this series, please visit: www.routledge.com/Routledge-Insights-in-Tourism-Series/book-series/RITS

Tourism, Knowledge and Learning

Edited by Eva Maria Jernsand, Maria Persson and Erik Lundberg

Routledge
Taylor & Francis Group
LONDON AND NEW YORK

First published 2023
by Routledge
4 Park Square, Milton Park, Abingdon, Oxon OX14 4RN

and by Routledge
605 Third Avenue, New York, NY 10158

*Routledge is an imprint of the Taylor & Francis Group, an informa
business*

British Library Cataloguing-in-Publication Data
A catalogue record for this book is available from the British Library

ISBN: 978-1-032-27488-1 (hbk)
ISBN: 978-1-032-27564-2 (pbk)
ISBN: 978-1-003-29331-6 (ebk)

DOI: 10.4324/9781003293316

Typeset in Times New Roman
by Apex CoVantage, LLC

Contents

Contributors

Axelsson, Anna
School of Global Studies, University of Gothenburg, Sweden

Gipperth, Lena
Department of Law, University of Gothenburg, Sweden

Hansen, Andreas Skriver
Department of Economy and Society, University of Gothenburg, Sweden

Jernsand, Eva Maria
Department of Business Administration, University of Gothenburg, Sweden

Lundberg, Erik
Department of Business Administration, University of Gothenburg, Sweden

Martinsson, Tyrone
HDK-Valand – Academy of Art and Design, University of Gothenburg, Sweden

Mellby, Clas
Department of Technology Management and Economics, Chalmers University of Technology, Sweden

Nilsson, Jan-Henrik
Department of Service Studies, Lund University, Sweden

Persson, Maria
Department of Historical Studies, University of Gothenburg, Sweden

Synnestvedt, Anita
Department of Historical Studies, University of Gothenburg, Sweden

Zillinger, Malin
Department of Service Studies, Lund University, Sweden

Preface

This is a book about tourism which, in different ways and forms, is based on knowledge mediation and learning activities. The idea of writing this book came from a perceived gap in the available literature touching upon this subject and also as a way of summarizing a two-year research project called "Knowledge tourism as attraction and resource" (2020–2022). This research project was generously funded by BFUF (the R&D Fund of the Swedish Tourism & Hospitality Industry) and organized by the principal researchers, who are also the editors of this book and who are active at the Centre for Tourism at the University of Gothenburg, Sweden. All but one of the chapters are written by researchers affiliated with universities in Gothenburg and coming from a broad variety of disciplines. Thus, many chapters draw on empirical material from the region of West Sweden (where Gothenburg is located), particularly connected to the project partners, which consist of research stations, cultural heritage sites, a municipality organization and a state administrative authority. However, the aim is to present conceptualizations, results and ultimately contributions that are valid outside of this geographical context.

1 An introduction

Learning and sustainable tourism

Eva Maria Jernsand, Maria Persson and Erik Lundberg

Relaxation, escapism and similar hedonic travel motives constitute the backbone of the contemporary tourism industry and a basis for a large part of tourism research (see Pearce & Lee, 2005). Other, more eudaemonic travel motives and interests, like learning and personal development, are often seen as more peripheral and a niche market for the tourism industry (Falk et al., 2012). However, a change is underway. Motives that were previously seen as peripheral are now gaining momentum, in line with societal and market changes. The transformation relates to the climate crisis, sustainable development, the Covid-19 crisis and travellers being more experienced, knowledgable and aware than ever before (see Schweinsberg & O'Flynn, 2022). For instance, numbers of pro-environment customers are rapidly growing, and these customers actively seek eco-friendly products during travel (Han & Hyun, 2017). Tourists want to achieve outcomes "related to their emotional status, learning opportunities or transformational occasions" (Volo, 2022, p. 554). Furthermore, rapid technological developments are providing new opportunities for learning and ways of discussing and sharing experiences, thus motivating sustainable behaviour and behavioural intentions (Han et al., 2018).

From a wider perspective, the challenges from global tragedies and effects of global change call for strategies to enhance sustainable development learning (Gössling, 2018) and collective learning, in order to transform the global tourism system and align it with the sustainability goals of the United Nations 2030 Agenda for Sustainable Development (Gössling et al., 2021). There are not only environmental threats to climate and biodiversity but also social threats to welfare, security and democracy (Hall, 2019; Scott et al., 2016), which must be addressed in collaboration between actors (Hall, 2019).

This book aims to contribute to the understanding of how tourism can be designed to provide conditions for learning. This involves learning for

DOI: 10.4324/9781003293316-1

tourists, the tourist industry, public authorities and local communities. We explore how tourism, knowledge and learning can be used as means towards sustainable development through current, new or changed structures, concepts, activities and communication efforts. As such, the book contributes to a better understanding of sustainable tourism as a direction, orientation or process for transforming social systems and behaviours; such approaches to tourism thereby contribute to sustainable development (Bramwell et al., 2017; Edgell Sr, 2019). The book should be seen as both an inspiration for tourism actors (e.g. tourism attractions, policy makers and other industry actors), and a scholarly contribution to further research tourism, knowledge and learning and the relationship between them. A holistic approach distinguishes this book from most existing literature that focuses on separate units of tourism – for instance, personal or community well-being, nature-based tourism, cultural heritage tourism or tourism that is a result of researchers' travels (so-called scientific tourism).

Theoretical perspectives

The book presents and contributes to theoretical, empirical and methodological approaches. The chapters are based in the theories of experiential learning (Kolb, 1984) and transformative learning (Mezirow, 1990). *Experience-based learning* emphasizes the importance of experiences: that learning is more effective when we reflect on actual experiences and use the experiences to understand or meet new situations. Experience-based learning is a learning philosophy inspired, for instance, by John Dewey's theory of experience from 1938. His work presented a holistic approach to learning and education based on the belief that we become part of and understand the world through experiences. Humans act in the world and it is in the action itself, in relation to and with the environment, that knowledge (and learning) arises. Further, knowledge gained this way is perceived as personally important, and may awaken our curiosity and even engage our emotions (Dewey, 1938; Synnestvedt, 2008). Other inspirations for Kolb's theory of experience-based learning are Lewin (1946), with his circles of planning, action and fact-finding, and Piaget (1952), with his "staircase" model of children's cognitive growth through interactions with their environment.

Kolb (1984) stated that the experiential learning cycle entails four stages: the concrete experience, a reflective observation, abstract conceptualization and active experimentation. In a tourism context, Falk and colleagues (2012) state that learning resulting from tourist experiences is personal and linked to the individual's personal interests and previous knowledge, as well as identity-related needs and expectations, including personal growth. We become more adventurous and gain more self-confidence the more experience we gain, and we want to further develop our skills and get answers to our questions (Savener, 2013). The experience logic, with its emotional approach, is also considered to have replaced the product and service logic, which rather satisfies material, logical and functional needs. Experiences are, for example, based on stories, rituals, symbolism, interaction and presence. Experiences that make us engage our senses and that create personal meaning therefore have greater potential to contribute to learning, simply because the experience inputs reach and are consumed on a deeper personal level (Falk et al., 2012). In tourism research, the experiential learning models of Kolb (1984) have been applied, for example, to understanding how augmented reality can enhance learning in cultural heritage tourism (Moorhouse et al., 2017), how to use virtual reality to enhance tourism students' learning in relation to the climate crisis (Schott, 2017) and how eco-tourism and wildlife tourism can use experience-based learning to make visitors adapt or change behaviours upon their return back home (Ballantyne & Packer, 2011).

Another central theoretical concept is *transformative learning*, which also comes from the educational sciences. Learning takes place in an "ongoing knowledge building process" (Gipps, 1999, p. 372) and the learning process therefore often has the ability to change thoughts, opinions, actions and worldviews (Mezirow, 1990; Reisinger, 2013). Knowledge also gives self-confidence, controls our actions and choices and helps us understand our own identity and role in society (Reisinger, 2015). According to Mezirow (2009), critical reflection is required for us to confront and begin to renegotiate our beliefs and assumptions, which in turn may cause us to change our actions and behaviours when we are reintegrated into society (i.e. back from our vacation, in the case of tourism). This transformative learning process has been adapted in tourism research to some extent, notably in relation to volunteer tourism (Coghlan & Gooch, 2011; Müller et al., 2020) and ecotourism (Walter, 2016; Sen & Walter, 2020). Räikkönen et al. (2021) also argues for the possibility of transformative learning experiences in the context of nature-based tourism.

In this book, and in accordance with Kolb's (1984) and Mezirow's (1990) theories, we assume that tourism experiences can contribute to transformative learning and ultimately lead to sustainable development as a result of increased personal and world awareness acquired by confrontation with and immersion in new knowledge as a result of travelling. Sustainable tourism as a concept has in recent decades developed to include not only ecological but also economic, cultural, social and political sustainable development through changes in behaviour and social systems (Bramwell et al., 2017). When different interests meet, goal conflicts are created, for example between conservation and development. Knowledge provides increased understanding and awareness of, for example, the value of the natural and cultural environment, or social vs. environmental needs. In this way, acquired knowledge contributes to an increased interest among both tourists and tourist actors in contributing to sustainable development, both individually and collectively. An important effect of this is increased protection of cultural and natural resources (Han & Hyun, 2017; Persson, 2019).

As tourists demand more learning experiences while travelling, there is a need to focus more consistently and strategically on tourism, knowledge and learning, including conceptual development and, not least, case studies examining the opportunities and challenges involved in producing and consuming high-quality knowledge-based tourist experiences. This book refers to tourism that in various ways has learning as a purpose. Learning experiences are designed or mediated to bring about or create conditions for learning. Such experiences form a large part of the tourism industry today, both in built environments such as museums, aquariums, zoos and science centers, and in natural, cultural or industrial environments such as culture and social heritage sites, nature reserves or national parks. A specific form is science tourism, which is tourism directly or indirectly linked to research activities. In some cases, the tourist can also contribute to research through his or her participation (so-called citizen science), which is a way to democratize knowledge through opening up rather closed research and expert knowledge and giving other people insight and opportunity to contribute to and even influence scientific knowledge.

Conceptual, empirical and methodological contributions to tourism, knowledge and learning

The book aims to inspire its readers to broaden and deepen collaboration across disciplinary, sectoral, cultural and social boundaries. The various contributors to the book provide a range of perspectives and experiences, from social sciences, with a focus on marketing, innovation management, human geography and environmental law; to arts and humanities, with a focus on heritage studies, archaeology and photography; and, finally, to natural sciences, with a focus on marine sciences. Working together on the book has increased our understanding of other ways of knowing and our discussions have contributed to the development of each chapter.

Following this brief introduction are six chapters with different perspectives on tourism, knowledge and learning. The concluding chapter comprises a summary and a research agenda. In chapter 2, four researchers (Jernsand, Hansen, Mellby and Gipperth) from different disciplines explore the potential of using UNESCO biosphere reserves (BRs) as platforms for sustainable destination development through transdisciplinary co-production of knowledge. Being involved in the initial phases of creating a BR themselves, the authors identify opportunities and obstacles involved, both in the BR setting and process. They give examples of existing initiatives in the study region and suggest measures for how BRs can become role models for knowledge building, sustainable development and addressing global challenges.

In chapter 3, Lundberg, Persson and Jernsand present a conceptualization of science tourism, a type of niche tourism that has learning and knowledge at its core. Previous research is scarce and science tourism is often treated as part of, for instance, ecotourism or educational tourism. In this chapter, the authors develop a model to understand the phenomenon from the perspective of the service provider (i.e. a producer perspective). The dimensions that are highlighted are the service provider's embeddedness in the tourism industry and in science, respectively, and how the providers, through their activities, enable tourists to immerse themselves in the activities.

The next three chapters (4, 5 and 6) discuss different types of mediation of knowledge in tourism contexts. In chapter 4, Zillinger and Nilsson discuss the role of the tour guide and the learning that takes place on guided tours. They apply a chronological perspective, starting with the Grand Tour in the 17th and 18th centuries, onwards to industrial Europe and post-war mass tourism, and thence to the role of the guide in today's digital era. Further, they explore how different guide roles have contributed to tourists' learning. The three theoretical learning concepts of episteme, techne and phronesis are used to examine the role of the guide. All three of these concepts matter on guided tours and enable tourists' learning.

In chapter 5, Persson and Synnestvedt explore information panels as communication channels for archaeological knowledge within the tourism spectra. An information panel is often the only channel of knowledge a visitor engages with at an archaeological site. Hence, the panel shapes visitors' learning experience of a site, and its content and layout are therefore of great importance. The concept of heritage interpretation is put forward as a way to facilitate experience-based learning through information panels, since it focuses on creating personal meaning for the tourist.

In chapter 6, Martinsson addresses the development of visual technologies as tools to aid learning through experiences. The focus is on the islands of Svalbard in the high Arctic, where tourist experiences include historical sites, spectacular landscapes and encounters with Arctic animals, but also encompass a landscape that is being altered by climate change. Recent developments in visual technologies open a new era of virtual travel and simulated nature experiences, which offer ways to experience the Arctic without actually going there. Visualizing, for instance, the historic development of melting ice through photos and virtual experiences can enhance transformational learning, democratize knowledge and reduce the risk of over-tourism in the Arctic.

One potential example of science tourism (as discussed in chapter 3) is citizen science. Axelsson and Hansen present this concept in chapter 7 and make connections to the tourism industry. Specifically, the authors show how an active use of citizen science has many positive characteristics and potentials that could be applied to create attractive tourism experiences. The authors exemplify this application in tourism with two cases: one on the use of tourist-produced pictures of important experience qualities, helping both scientific and management practices, and one on local beach cleaning activities and their educational potential.

Finally, chapter 8 synthesizes the learnings of each chapter in the book in order to provide the reader both with avenues for further research and with practical insights for managing learning processes and knowledge creation in a tourism context.

References

Ballantyne, R., & Packer, J. (2011). Using tourism free-choice learning experiences to promote environmentally sustainable behaviour: The role of post-visit 'action resources'. *Environmental Education Research*, 17(2), 201–215. https://doi.org/1 0.1080/13504622.2010.530645

Bramwell, B., Higham, J., Lane, B., & Miller, G. (2017). Twenty-five years of sustainable tourism and the journal of sustainable tourism: Looking back and moving forward. *Journal of Sustainable Tourism*, 25(1), 1–9. https://doi.org/10.1080/096 69582.2017.1251689

Coghlan, A., & Gooch, M. (2011). Applying a transformative learning framework to volunteer tourism. *Journal of Sustainable Tourism*, 19(6), 713–728. https://doi.org/10.1080/09669582.2010.542246

Dewey, J. (1938/1997). *Experience and Education*. [New ed.]. New York: Simon & Schuster.

Edgell Sr, D. L. (2019). *Managing Sustainable Tourism: A Legacy for the Future*. New York: Routledge.

Falk, J. H., Ballantyne, R., Packer, J., & Benckendorff, P. (2012). Travel and learning: A neglected tourism research area. *Annals of Tourism Research*, 39(2), 908–927. https://doi.org/10.1016/j.annals.2011.11.016

Gipps, C. (1999). Socio-cultural aspects of assessment. *Review of Research in Education*, 24(1), 355–392.

Gössling, S. (2018). Tourism, tourist learning and sustainability: An exploratory discussion of complexities, problems and opportunities. *Journal of Sustainable Tourism*, 26(2), 292–306. https://doi.org/10.1080/09669582.2017.1349772

Gössling, S., Scott, D., & Hall, C. M. (2021). Pandemics, tourism and global change: A rapid assessment of COVID-19. *Journal of Sustainable Tourism*, 29(1), 1–20. https://doi.org/10.1080/09669582.2020.1758708

Hall, C. M. (2019). Constructing sustainable tourism development: The 2030 agenda and the managerial ecology of sustainable tourism, *Journal of Sustainable Tourism*, 27(7), 1044–1060. https://doi.org/10.1080/09669582.2018.1560456

Han, H., & Hyun, S. S. (2017). Fostering customers' proenvironmental behavior at a museum. *Journal of Sustainable Tourism*, 25(9), 1240–1256. https://doi.org/10. 1080/09669582.2016.1259318

Han, W., McCabe, S., Wang, Y., & Chong, A. Y. L. (2018). Evaluating user-generated content in social media: An effective approach to encourage greater pro-environmental behavior in tourism? *Journal of Sustainable Tourism*, 26(4), 600–614. https://doi.org/10.1080/09669582.2017.1372442

Kolb, D. (1984). *Experiential Learning: Experience as the Source of Learning and Development*. Englewood Cliffs, NJ: Prentice Hall.

Lewin, K. (1946). Action research and minority problems. *Journal of Social Issues*, 2(4), 34–46

Mezirow, J. (1990). How critical reflection triggers transformative learning. *Fostering Critical Reflection in Adulthood*, 1(20), 1–6.

Mezirow, J. (2009). An overview of transformative learning. In K. Illeris (Ed.), *Contemporary Theories of Learning: Learning Theorists in Their Own Words* (pp. 90–105). New York: Routledge.

Moorhouse, N., Tom Dieck, M., & Jung, T. (2017). Augmented Reality to enhance the learning experience in cultural heritage tourism: An experiential learning cycle perspective. *eReview of Tourism Research*, 8, https://agrilife.org/ertr/files/2016/12/RN58.pdf

Müller, C. V., Scheffer, A. B. B., & Closs, L. Q. (2020). Volunteer tourism, transformative learning and its impacts on careers: The case of Brazilian volunteers. *International Journal of Tourism Research*, 22(6), 726–738, https://doi.org/10.1002/jtr.2368

Pearce, P. L., & Lee, U.-I. (2005). Developing the travel career approach to tourist motivation. *Journal of Travel Research*, 43(3), 226–237, https://doi.org/10.1177%2F0047287504272020

Persson, M. (2019). Science tourism och kunskapsturismens möjligheter. *Delrapport 3. Kunskapsturism. Maritim utveckling i Bohuslän*. www.tillvaxtbohuslan.se/wp-content/uploads/2019/10/v.5-FINAL-Tryckfil-2019-10-08-Rapport-Kunskapsturism-Delrapport-3.pdf

Piaget, J. (1952). Jean Piaget. In E. G. Boring, H. Werner, H. S. Langfeld, & R. M. Yerkes (Eds.), *A History of Psychology in Autobiography* (vol. 4, pp. 237–256). Worcester, MA: Clark University Press. https://doi.org/10.1037/11154-011

Räikkönen, J., Grénman, M., Rouhiainen, H., Honkanen, A., & Sääksjärvi. I. E. (2021). Conceptualizing nature-based science tourism: A case study of Seili Island, Finland. *Journal of Sustainable Tourism*. https://doi.org/10.1080/09669 582.2021.1948553

Reisinger, Y. (2013). Preface. In Y. Reisinger (Ed.), *Transformational Tourism: Tourist Perspectives* (pp. xii–xiv). Wallingford: CABI. http://dx.doi.org/10.1079/9781780642093.0000

8   *Eva Maria Jernsand et al.*

Reisinger. Y. (2015). Reflections on life purpose. In Y. Reisinger (Ed.), *Transformational Tourism: Host Perspectives* (pp. 3–5). Wallingford: CABI. http://dx.doi.org/10.1079/9781780643922.0000

Savener, A. (2013). Finding themselves in San Blas, Panama. In Y. Reisinger (Ed.), *Transformational Tourism: Tourist Perspectives* (pp. 136–148). Wallingford: CABI. http://dx.doi.org/10.1079/9781780642093.0000

Schott, C. (2017). Virtual fieldtrips and climate change education for tourism students. *Journal of Hospitality, Leisure, Sport & Tourism Education*, 21, 13–22. https://doi.org/10.1016/j.jhlste.2017.05.002

Schweinsberg, S., & O'Flynn, L. (2022). Ecotourist experience: Myth or reality? In R. Sharpley (Ed.), *Routledge Handbook of the Tourist Experience* (pp. 286–300). Abingdon and New York: Routledge. https://doi.org/10.4324/9781003219866

Scott, D., Hall, C. M., & Gössling, S. (2016). A review of the IPCC 5th Assessment and implications for tourism sector climate resilience and decarbonization. *Journal of Sustainable Tourism*, 24(1), 8–30. https://doi.org/10.1080/09669582.2015.1062021

Sen, V., & Walter, P. (2020). Community-based ecotourism and the transformative learning of homestay hosts in Cambodia. *Tourism Recreation Research*, 45(3), 323–336. https://doi.org/10.1080/02508281.2019.1692171

Synnestvedt, A. (2008). *Fornlämningsplatsen: kärleksaffär eller trist historia*. Diss. Gothenburg: University of Gothenburg.

Volo, S. (2022). Tourist experience: A marketing perspective. In R. Sharpley (Ed.), *Routledge Handbook of the Tourist Experience* (pp. 549–563). Abingdon and New York: Routledge.

Walter, P. G. (2016). Catalysts for transformative learning in community-based ecotourism. *Current Issues in Tourism*, 19(13), 1356–1371. https://doi.org/10.1080/13683500.2013.850063

2 Destination development based on knowledge and learning

Initiating a UNESCO biosphere reserve in Bohuslän

Eva Maria Jernsand, Andreas Skriver Hansen, Clas Mellby and Lena Gipperth

Personal enrichment and learning are motivating factors for travel (e.g. Shoemaker, 1994; Su et al., 2018) and, as stated in chapter 1, travel and tourism can change people's thoughts, opinions, actions and worldviews and thereby be agents of change for sustainable development. Learning and knowledge are also important aspects of destination development on a local and regional scale, being central to collaborative decision-making processes, innovation and sustainability (Habibah et al., 2013; Hoppstadius, 2018; Schianetz et al., 2009). To address societal challenges, transdisciplinary co-production of knowledge is often put forward as an appropriate approach, since it involves logic, understanding and perspectives from academia and the public, private and civic sectors. Transdisciplinary processes include identifying and including stakeholders and disciplines, and integrating their different types of knowledge (Gibbons et al., 1994; Polk & Kain, 2015). For this purpose, and in relation to destination development, a substantial platform and infrastructure is needed that develops and facilitates transdisciplinary co-production of knowledge and, as a result, public education and engagement through tourism and leisure. This chapter argues that the UNESCO Man and Biosphere (MAB) concept offers such a platform and infrastructure.

The MAB program was initiated in 1971 and has since expanded to include a world network of 727 biosphere reserves (BRs) across 131 countries (UNESCO, 2021a). The common objective is to support biodiversity, cultural diversity and conservation, as well as advancing sustainability, scientific research and public education (Reed & Price, 2020a; UNESCO, 1996; UNESCO, 2021b). Moreover, BRs are popular tourist destinations in many parts of the world, and they are important sources of income for residents (Těšitela & Kušová, 2020; Bires & Raj, 2020). One of the arguments for the MAB

DOI: 10.4324/9781003293316-2

program is ecological and cultural education through sustainable tourism (Shaw et al., 2020; UNESCO, 1996). Also, as Bouamrane et al. (2020, p. 40) note, today, BRs are "increasingly embedded in global initiatives, and play important roles as models of sustainable development at regional and national scales." This means that BRs serve as learning sites, translating the global principles of sustainable development into locally relevant praxis on the ground. For this reason, local collaboration and dialogue is essential throughout the BR process, a perspective shared by Bires and Raj (2020), who propose a holistic view with linkages between BR development plans and destination development plans, with a focus on involving local communities in tourism development initiatives and activities. At the same time, few studies have specifically explored how BRs can work as platforms and generators for developing destinations with a focus on sharing knowledge and learning activities, and where various stakeholders are involved in initiating, inventing and developing such a process (Habibah et al., 2013).

This chapter aims to address this situation and knowledge gap by using a case study and action research approach. The purpose is to explore the BR concept and its potential as a platform for sustainable-destination development with a focus on transdisciplinary knowledge co-production. After a short section on methodology follows a theoretical framework on collaborative concepts related to destination development and transdisciplinary work, particularly focused on BRs. This is followed by the example of Bohuslän, a province located on Sweden's west coast, where the authors have been involved in the initial phases of developing a BR, which at the time of writing is still at the application stage. In this work, we first give examples of existing tourism, knowledge and learning initiatives in the region. Hereafter, the collaborative process of the making of the BR in Bohuslän is described and analyzed in order to discuss how the proposed BR can be developed to become a suitable platform for developing destinations through transdisciplinary knowledge co-production.

Methodology

The authors were part of the BR process in Bohuslän during its initial phase as the project's steering group and led a feasibility study, including the development of action plans and their implementation. The authors also took an active part in the feasability study workshops (for detailed method descriptions, see WSP, 2020). Thus, the research methodology was qualitative and action-oriented. This qualitative approach makes the research robust through in-depth insights into the studied phenomena, for instance by addressing issues beyond the specific case (Coghlan & Shani, 2014). Action research – that is, the simultaneous process of taking action and doing research – was chosen as the best way to achieve the aims of this study, as it contributes to making research societally relevant, with a focus on change and the creation of practice-based knowledge on the ground (Coghlan & Shani, 2014). The transdisciplinary approach promoted, involving actors from various regional and local sectors and disciplines, was also used by the authors and their partners in the study, which further strengthens the methodology used.

Theoretical framework

A transdisciplinary approach to destination development

Traditional framings for destination management, governance and leadership have been impacted and challenged by broader conceptualizations of sustainable development, where global societal challenges push for advancements in tourism research and practice (Volgger et al., 2021). Threats to, for instance, climate, biodiversity, welfare, security and democracy call for multiple angles, directions and interpretations (Hall, 2019; Scott et al., 2016). In this vein, sustainable tourism is defined as a process of transforming systems and behaviours (Bramwell et al., 2017; Edgell Sr, 2019) and thereby changes the focus from tourism to sustainability (Saarinen, 2013). As such, traditional narrow views of partnerships, competitiveness and networks in tourism (Hall, 2019; Volgger et al., 2021) require reconsideration to include a larger set of actors, knowledges and social locations (Hall, 2019), transcending scientific disciplines and methodologies (Bramwell et al., 2017).

Transdisciplinary approaches bring together partnerships and networks of public, private and civic sectors, including academia, with their different perspectives, logics and understandings (Gibbons et al., 1994; Polk & Kain, 2015). Specifically, transdisciplinary processes address democracy, inclusiveness and sustainability (Polk & Kain, 2015), and they stretch across disciplines (Guggenheim, 2006). Furthermore, transdisciplinarity is said to be a way of tackling so-called wicked problems (Pohl et al., 2017), which have mutual dependencies, are contradictory and complex, and have no single solution, while the resources needed to solve them often change over time (Rittel & Webber, 1973). In order to work towards destinations that have the capacity to address global challenges, using a transdisciplinary approach is therefore not only helpful, but may in fact be the only way to achieve this.

Transdisciplinary approaches in biosphere reserves

A central idea in the transdisciplinary approach is that problems should be defined and collaboratively dealt with in specific and localized contexts

(Gibbons et al., 1994). BRs can be seen as such identified contexts, and in fact, transdisciplinarity is often used in descriptions of BRs as an approach to "learn about and reconcile human-environment relations," becoming "a test-bed for applying sustainability science on the ground" (Reed & Price, 2020b, p. 321). In BRs, people can seek collaborations across sectors and scales for mutual learning, benefits and measures at higher levels, as well as experiment with and demonstrate strategies for sustainability (Reed & Price, 2020b). Transdisciplinary approaches are, for instance, used in the implementation of new actions in BRs (Onaindia et al., 2020), for the reactivation of BRs (Matsuda et al., 2020), and for the inclusion of academia in the development and governance of BRs (Walk et al., 2020).

However, as Kjellqvist and colleagues (2020) note from BRs in Sweden, in the initial phases, before the BRs are nominated for inclusion in the MAB program, few types of knowledge (scientific, expert/technical and lay/local) tend to be used. Moreover, researchers often approach BRs from above, doing research "on" rather than "with" organizations and communities. Also challenging is how "knowledge domains" from conservation and natural science (e.g. municipal ecologists) are often predominant in the BR nomination process, while social scientists (e.g. economists and human geographers) are often underrepresented. As such, the significant learning opportunities that come with BRs call for a transdisciplinary approach with a focus on broader partnerships, across disciplines, sectors, levels and departments, and the inclusion of all these in the early phases of creating a BR (Kjellqvist et al., 2020). In the following, Bohuslän is used as an example to showcase how local and regional stakeholders are already collaborating around developing destinations, but where a clear model to include the learning and knowledge capacities needed in today's global context is missing.

Bohuslän as a learning destination

Bohuslän is a province that stretches from Sweden's second largest city, Gothenburg, in the south, to the Norwegian border in the north (see Figure 2.1), and is a well-known destination for regional and national as well as international tourists. The population in Bohuslän is about 310,000, but there is also a large group of seasonal residents. The province has more than 1 million commercial overnight stays a year (an average during the period 2018–2020), most of them (about 90–95%) from Sweden and Norway (Ranefjärd 2018, 2019, 2020). In the Västra Götaland region, to which Bohuslän belongs, live another 1.4 million, the majority in Gothenburg.

This is not the first time Bohuslän has been considered important to safeguard and develop within a sustainable framework and as a learning

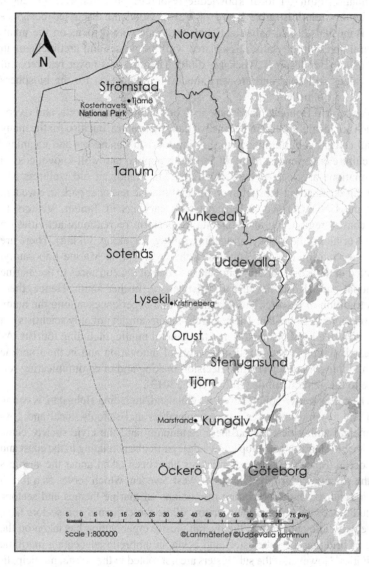

Figure 2.1 The province of Bohuslän consists of 12 municipalities in an area of 4,400 km². All municipalities have direct access to the coastline but also include inland areas.

Source: ©*Uddevalla municipality and* ©*Lantmäteriet*

(Lantmäteriet is an authority belonging to the Swedish Ministry of Finance, responsible for the division of real estate in Sweden. It provides the public sector, businesses and individuals with information on geography and real estate.)

destination built on local knowledge resources. In a report from 2000, the county administrative board of Västra Götaland discussed designating Bohuslän as a so-called national landscape with a focus on the many natural and cultural values associated with the coasts and archipelagos in Bohuslän (Bondeson & Wockatz, 2000). The idea was never realized, but the values still exist and are very much the foundation for the biosphere reserve in Bohuslän.

The typical Bohuslän landscape includes archipelagos, fjords and rivers, which are ideal for tourism because of their rich nature, but also for the many small coastal communities with thriving tourism businesses and meaningful culture experiences. Many of Sweden's popular and well-known coastal destinations are located here, including Marstrand, an old wellness and boating destination; Kosterhavet, the first marine national park in Sweden; and the UNESCO World Heritage rock carvings in Tanum. Visitors to the coastal region, but also inhabitants, perform recreational activities on shore or along the coast (e.g. fishing, sailing, kayaking, hiking). There are also two marine research stations in the area: Tjärnö Marine Laboratory, located in the Koster archipelago close to one of the entrances to the marine national park, Kosterhavet, and Kristineberg, further south. Hence, there is a tradition of research-based activities and experiences among the many destinations in Bohuslän. The research stations attract not only scientists but also schools, local businesses and the general public, including tourists. As research stations, they are also hotspots of innovation and in the frontline both of integrating science into decision-making and of communicating science to the general public (Billick et al., 2013).

The collaborative culture in Västra Götaland, including Bohuslän, is strong and has fostered processes where universities and schools, local and governmental authorities, the business community and the civic society come together to share and develop knowledge, particularly relating to the coast and the ocean. Since 2012, many initiatives have been taken under the auspices of the so-called Maritime Cluster of West Sweden, which serves as a forum for specialized and crosscutting discussions on marine themes and sectors, including coastal and marine tourism. While these themes and sectors have developed into subclusters, the overall cluster organization has taken on the role of bridging the subclusters and being an umbrella advocating maritime activities. However, if the subclusters are not rooted in the coastal municipalities, the whole cluster risks being a network of experts without sufficient ways to bring the many common interests together. Launching the BR can be a way of giving local initiatives a regional context and provide a necessary rejuvenation of the cluster as a platform for collaboration.

Also relevant is the Maritime Action Program for Västra Götaland, established in 2015, which has given incentives to further strengthen the focus on sustainability in the development of the coastal zone of Bohuslän (Region Västra Götaland, 2016). The focus of the strategy, which is one of the many inspirations in the making of the BR in Bohuslän, is on: 1) maintaining and developing maritime competence and competitiveness, 2) collaborating across sector and industry boundaries, 3) collaborating in long-term partnerships with participation from business, academia and institutes as well as public actors including municipalities and state authorities, and 4) influencing and interacting with the national, European and international maritime agendas. In this regard, it is noteworthy that the regional, and later the national, maritime strategy for development have both promoted the development of joint collaboration in research and innovation. Moreover, on a local level, municipal collaboration, such as recent work on creating a thematic blue plan in addition to local municipal plans in northern Bohuslän, has been a driver of transdisciplinary collaboration. Interestingly, the plan emphasizes that there are good conditions for the development of research-community couplings and that the research anchored in local businesses and communities must be maintained and developed. At the same time, translating both the maritime strategies and the blue plan into action, including how to create and anchor research-community couplings, has met with some difficulties among the many (especially local) stakeholders, such as municipalities and coastal businesses and organizations. A central challenge is funding, as well as the competences and personnel needed to work with these initiatives. A BR would be a way of securing all three aspects and thus a way of strengthening existing processes at the local level.

Central to all of the initiatives mentioned is an emphasis on learning, such as learning within and across levels, but also learning through collaboration in planning and in specific activities, including tourism and destination initiatives. Bohuslän (and the region as a whole) has developed an informal learning environment that connects political visions and strategies with business life and livelihoods on a local level. The informal learning environment is highly effective in destination development and management and is thus one of the core aspects promoted in the proposed BR. For example, a large number of research projects are designed to establish and promote in-depth collaboration between local public and private actors while aiming for the sustainable development of the Bohuslän coast. Also, over the years, there has been a focus on increasing knowledge about important marine resources and ecosystems, the impacts of human-imposed pressures such as climate change and conditions for sustainable business development in sectors such as tourism. Combining all these aspects are a number of projects defining hurdles and drivers to develop more sustainable leisure boating in the area (University of Gothenburg, n.d.).

Other initiatives include citizen science activities, combining science needs with environmental education and Sweden's first marine allotment, a cultivation area in the sea with the aim of growing and storing raw foods from the sea on a small scale. Important stakeholders include both households and small businesses like restaurants, while the process also helps to promote learning about species and marine ecosystems. Finally, the Tjärnö Marine Laboratory has a long tradition of welcoming visitors almost all year round to guided tours (including their public aquariums), beach excursions and research vessel excursions. In the summer, there is also a series of popular science lectures and children's camps. The twin research station Kristineberg provides scientific support to the saltwater aquarium Havets Hus, one of the key destinations in Bohuslän, but also attracts a large number of visitors in itself, particularly during the West Coast Maritime Week (Region Västra Götaland, n.d.), a yearly celebration of the west coast's environment and culture.

While there are certainly many good initiatives and activities in the region, there are also challenges to point out, like the case of the Maritime Cluster and local work on the maritime visions and blue plans. Indeed, there are initiatives and collaborations that do not take place, ambitions that remain unfulfilled and unestablished and tacit knowledge that remains hidden. In this section, we have given attention to existing qualities, but we also need to acknowledge that there are areas for improvement. For example, the different administrative levels and responsibilities within the region are a challenge, as they can put a stop to initiatives and intentions, and for a multitude of other reasons. Another example is the management of the coastal-marine environment, on which there is a lot of focus but little coordination so far. Furthermore, a large number of projects also strive to fulfill one or more goals stated in the 2030 Agenda for Sustainable Development, many relating to tourism. However, they are often scattered and lack sufficient infrastructure to bridge experiences, competencies and knowledge. Consequently, what perhaps is missing the most in the plethora of ongoing related collaborations and initiatives is organization. Specifically, there is a need for professional coordination and communication on local and regional levels. And above all, there is a need for systems improvement in all of Bohuslän.

The collaborative BR process in Bohuslän

The initiative to create a BR in Bohuslän came in 2019 from Uddevalla, one of the municipalities in Bohuslän. The idea had emerged during an earlier project on a regional master plan as a possible solution to increase the sustainability of the tourist industry in Bohuslän. The idea of a BR also coincided with the reconciliation phase of the maritime cluster of West Sweden. Hence, a group of stakeholders initiated a dialogue about a potential BR in Bohuslän. The group consisted of the University of Gothenburg, Uddevalla, Lysekil and Munkedal municipalities and Leader Bohuskust och gränsbygd (a non-profit European Union–funded public benefit association that supports rural and marine development in Bohuslän). A steering group was formed, with representatives from the University of Gothenburg, Uddevalla and Lysekil municipalities, Leader Bohuskust och gränsbygd and (somewhat later in the process) the two municipal associations in Bohuslän, which met regularly during the feasibility study. With backgrounds and competences in legislation, human geography, marine science, business administration, technology and other disciplines, the steering group got acquainted with the concept of BRs, with each other as individuals, and with their roles in their respective organizations. The steering group applied for funding of a feasibility study to investigate the prerequisites for a BR within the MAB program. A consultancy firm was assigned to carry out the study over a 12-month period (WSP, 2020). During the feasibility study, representatives from the steering group were involved in all activities as presenters, observers and discussants, and contributed by providing information to the consultants about key people in the networks so that they could contact potential participants and invite them to workshops.

The feasibility study included the identification of natural and cultural resources, knowledge actors and local engagement in projects. A set of interviews and dialogue meetings with stakeholders were held with the purpose of informing them about the initiative and identifying commitments and challenges in matters relating to sustainable development. During these activities, the stakeholders discussed the feasibility of a BR as a collaboration platform for coordination and dialogue, for receiving support for new and established projects and, most importantly, as an instrument for the transdisciplinary co-production of knowledge.

A total of four dialogue meetings were held with 12 associations and organizations:

* four community associations
* two fishing associations
* one museum
* one regional heritage association
* one foundation for public benefit
* one border committee for border municipalities and regions in Norway and Sweden
* one archipelago tour company
* one non-profit association supporting rural and marine development

Nine interviews were held with:

- an archipelago council
- an algae farming company
- a foundation for conservation, guiding and beach cleaning activities
- a business association
- a municipality association
- a centre for collaboration on innovation, business, education and employment
- the cultural and regional development administrations and the tourism board of the region

To prepare further work, study visits to other BRs in Sweden were organized, and for one person in the steering group, also to South Africa. From South Africa, it was found that tourism and regenerative farming are crucial themes for the BRs there. The main goal for visiting the Swedish BRs was to better understand the application process, as well as the purpose and the organization of the BRs. We found out that the application process is more about shaping the coming BR than about the writing itself. For most of the BRs in Sweden, the purpose centres on environmental issues, local community development, landscape conservation and similar issues. Only a few BRs have tourism as the reason and basis for their formation. One BR stands out, stemming from a conflict between landowners and nature conservation organizations. The landowners were worried about decreased possibilities of using the land while the nature conservation organizations wanted to protect red-listed species. The BR emerged from a dialogue process intended to solve the conflict. Today, however, all of the BRs have tourism on the agenda. For Bohuslän, which is an established tourist destination, one outcome of the whole process was to further explore the potential for developing the BR as a learning destination. Furthermore, the feasibility study revealed some points that required attention.

First, it demonstrated a need for increased communication of research results vis-à-vis business and local communities, which would benefit learning and be in line with the intentions of the BR. The study also points to the constant need to develop and deepen forms of collaboration, including destination development, and the potential of a BR process in structuring the further development of local collaboration initiatives. Furthermore, the BR is seen as a tool for prioritizing support and resources in development work, where collaboration between different types of organizations is needed and can potentially lead to greater efficiency if managed as a whole. Within the BR, existing local, regional, national and international policies, plans and governing documents on sustainable development would therefore be compiled, linked and integrated. In short, the BR would provide a broader, more holistic picture of the challenges and opportunities that exist in the BR area and a platform to work with them.

Second, the understanding of "biosphere reserve" was generally low and the term was perceived by the vast majority as a complicated and misleading concept. The name risks hampering a constructive dialogue, since it emphasizes the protection and conservation of biodiversity and natural areas more than collaboration, community development and place attraction. This indicates that a name would be preferable that can be used independently of the term "biosphere reserve", but which still informs people about the place in focus and preferably something about the content. Good examples of this include "Water Kingdom" and "Blekinge Archipelago" in southern Sweden, names that indicate they operate independently, compared to, for instance, "Vindelälven-Juhttátahkka's biosphere reserve." It is also important to communicate the content, purpose and structure of the BR through continuous dialogues with local and regional stakeholders, not least in the next stages of the process. A suggestion here is to use existing communication and action platforms, such as the research stations and the Maritime Cluster, to engage with and explain what the establishment of the BR will contribute, and specifically how it will benefit local and regional development initiatives. All of this should be done with a focus on creating the province as a hub for learning through transdisciplinary knowledge co-production.

Third, the feasibility study showed that success is born when local forces experience ownership of the process, as opposed to directives "from above." Some representatives also emphasized the importance of being clear on whether the BR is primarily aimed at municipal officials or the civic population. Considering previously failed top-down processes along the coastal zone in Bohuslän, many stakeholders found the democratic aspect of the Man and Biosphere programme appealing and pointed out the importance of anchoring the work in local communities. Therefore, the recruitment of local community representatives in the process is considered crucial for its development and success, and fits well with one of the main principles in the establishment of a BR: citizen involvement. Indeed, this is often the only way to secure a legitimate, just and equitable process. Once that is established, there is a higher chance of success as the initiative is founded and anchored in local knowledge and aspirations.

Fourth, most of the participants and interviewees were positive about the proposed BR idea, while a few were hesitant. A common comment was, "We already do this," which indicates that the added value of a BR was either not made clear or was not significant to some stakeholders. This issue must clearly be addressed, not least in the further BR process, in order not to confuse the overarching structure with existing and similar initiatives in the area, such as test beds for marine technologies, marine allotment gardens, mussel farming, research on bluefin tuna and many others. All these examples are the result of extensive collaboration between several very diverse local and regional actors. Thus, each stakeholder must be thoroughly introduced to the difference between existing initiatives and what value the BR will add. The BR should be seen as the umbrella that identifies, collects and communicates the different initiatives, that supports new initiatives and that brings stakeholders together for the co-production of new knowledge.

BRs as transdisciplinary platforms for destination development

With breadth and cutting-edge expertise, access to a unique marine infrastructure and coastal habitats and established cross-sector networks, we find that there are good conditions for continued and developed transdisciplinary co-production of knowledge in Bohuslän. At present, there is also a general optimism in the region, with people being energized and keen to commence and drive forward new initiatives. This is a factor that should not be underestimated, but it is also tricky, as the current momentum could disappear fast if it is not anchored properly and soon.

The already established learning environments in Bohuslän have developed as a result of transdisciplinary approaches. There are also various initiatives and projects where collaboration between actors on different levels is central and thus of importance for further development. In addition to this, the support from the various regional and national strategies, along with the general goals of the 2030 Agenda, gives further incentives to establish a BR in Bohuslän. For example, a 2018 report from the Maritime Cluster states, among other things, that there is a good basis for further development of contacts between researchers and companies in the region with a focus on the future commercial development of innovations.

A biosphere region would also be a way to frame smaller initiatives promoting sustainability. At a time when innovation and transformation is called for on a global, European, national and regional level, small projects or activities might not be visible and also risk being regarded as having low ambitions. Together and under a common frame, as suggested here with the BR, it is possible to work towards establishing a vivid region, where the initiatives of business and civic society can be supported by local and regional governments. Furthermore, areas that are administratively divided, such as the Bohuslän coast, seldom address common needs consistently. Thus, the establishment of a BR is a good opportunity to come together, learn from each other and bring important opportunities and challenges to the table.

Furthermore, a BR is a way of keeping current activities and processes alive and running, with the benefit of creating learning destinations that can utilize, and thereby pioneer, transdisciplinary knowledge co-production on a destination level. Because tourism is seen as a strength of Bohuslän – as emphasized throughout this chapter – a transdisciplinary platform like the BR opens up new avenues through which tourism can contribute to sustainability by changing systems and behaviours.

However, there is the potential for much more. For instance, future directions should look more at, and include, system changes to coordinate and communicate new initiatives and to explore collaboration and commitment in a more long-term perspective. This work should begin even in the initial phases of establishing a BR. Transdisciplinary approaches to destination development are relatively unexplored areas in tourism studies, especially the involvement of natural scientists. In BRs, on the other hand, broader partnerships with social scientists are often missing, especially in the initial phases. To avoid this scenario, the BR steering group used an action-oriented and transdisciplinary research approach during its efforts to establish a BR in Bohuslän; this approach can serve as inspiration for future constellations.

In the feasibility study, we also involved various stakeholders, both in the steering group and in the interviews and workshops, including municipalities, business and community associations, academia and various profit and non-profit tourism actors. We found good examples and realized the potential of the BR as a learning destination, with ongoing dialogue and co-production of knowledge among actors as the main focus and driver. However, it became clear that there is rarely only one problem and one solution. Rather, different perspectives of an issue raise new issues, goal conflicts and contradictions that must be addressed. This complexity, an ever-changing reality, referred to in the concept of "wicked problems," makes ongoing collaboration, dialogue and long-term perspectives all the more crucial. Future work should look more into how collaboration through dialogue meetings and interviews, where a variety of local and official actors participate, can be encouraged to continue as formal collaboration in the forthcoming BR in Bohuslän. This is a crucial aspect, as these, as well as other local actors and stakeholders yet to be included, are central for the development and success of the BR. As such, and as this work has only just started, we see another major task in anchoring not only the BR idea but also the learning environments required to successfully drive the fundamental principles of BRs forward.

Lastly, we believe that the BR can become a platform for project support and the integration of governing policies and plans. This includes working across different authority levels, as well as the inclusion of local communities, in order to succeed. However, communicating a concept such as the biosphere reserve and its potentials is not an easy task. The name itself does not signal collaboration or bottom-up initiatives and again, therefore, clear incentives for local community representatives are crucial so that the BR does not become yet another project for municipalities and officials. If the aspect of democracy is not fully integrated and supported by all stakeholders, the BR risks failure.

Conclusion

The "decade of action" to achieve the 2030 Agenda goals by the target date has more than begun. All sectors of society are called upon to renew ambitions, mobilization, leadership and collective action to achieve the required 2030 transformations (UN, 2019, 2021). However, although all sectors of society are putting efforts into fulfilling the 17 global sustainability goals, the complexity of factors influencing the systems and our behaviour as individuals has proven hard to tackle. In this chapter, we have demonstrated some aspects of this complexity, and have emphasized the transdisciplinary co-production of knowledge in UNESCO biosphere reserves (BRs) as a role model for sustainable development in line with the 2030 Agenda. Theoretically, and from our findings, we argue that a BR can constitute an optimal infrastructure for building and managing learning destinations. Moreover, we see significant potential in BRs for merging local and regional interests, which in turn contributes to the democratization of knowledge. Thus, the transdisciplinary approach forms a basis for inclusiveness and the co-production of knowledge for the purpose of facilitating conditions for learning, innovation and attractive destinations, while also addressing global challenges. Hence, BRs are well suited as examples of possible ways to transcend narrow views of partnerships, competitiveness and networks, and to be part of changing systems and behaviours.

References

Billick, I., Babb, I,, Kloeppel, B., Leong, J. C., Hodder, J., Sanders, J., & Swain, H. (2013). Field stations and marine laboratories of the future: A strategic vision. *National Association of Marine Laboratories and Organization of Biological Field Stations.* www.obfs.org/fsml-future.

Bires, Z., & Raj, S. (2020). Tourism as a pathway to livelihood diversification: Evidence from biosphere reserves, Ethiopia. *Tourism Management*, 81. https://doi.org/10.1016/j.tourman.2020.104159

Bondeson, R., & Wockatz, G. (2000). *Kustområdet och skärgården i Bohuslän – en värdebeskrivning av ett nationallandskap enligt 4 kap i miljöbalken.* Göteborg: Länsstyrelsen Västra Götaland.

Bouamrane, M., Dogsé, P., & Price, M. F. (2020). Biosphere reserves from Seville, 1995, to building a new world for 2030. In M. G. Reed & M. F. Martin (Eds.), *UNESCO Biosphere Reserves: Supporting Biocultural Diversity, Sustainability and Society* (pp. 29–44). London and New York: Routledge.

Bramwell, B., Higham, J., Lane, B., & Miller, G. (2017). Twenty-five years of sustainable tourism and the Journal of Sustainable Tourism: Looking back and moving forward. *Journal of Sustainable Tourism,* 25(1), 1–9. https://doi.org/10.1080/09669582.2017.1251689

Coghlan, D., & Shani, A. B. (2014). Creating action research quality in organization development: Rigorous, reflective and relevant. *Systemic practice and action research,* 27(6), 523–536.

Edgell Sr, D. L. (2019). *Managing Sustainable Tourism: A Legacy for the Future.* London and New York: Routledge.

Gibbons, M., Limoges, C., Nowotny, H., Schwartzman, S., Scott, P., & Trow, M. (1994). *The New Production of Knowledge: The Dynamics of Science and Research in Contemporary Societies.* London, Thousand Oaks, CA, New Delhi: Sage.

Guggenheim, M. (2006). Undisciplined research: The proceduralisation of quality control in transdisciplinary projects. *Science and Public Policy,* 33(6), 411–421. https://doi.org/10.3152/147154306781778795

Habibah, A., Mushrifah, I., Hamzah, J., Buang, A., Toriman, M. E., Abdullah, S. R. S., Nur Amirah, K. Z., Nur Farahin, Z., & Er, A. C. (2013). Biosphere reserve as a learning tourism destination: Approaches from Tasik Chini. *International Journal of Geosciences,* 4, 1447–1458. https://doi.org/10.4236/ijg.2013.410142

Hall, C. M. (2019). Constructing sustainable tourism development: The 2030 agenda and the managerial ecology of sustainable tourism. *Journal of Sustainable Tourism,* 27(7), 1044–1060. https://doi.org/10.1080/09669582.2018.1560456

Hoppstadius, F. (2018). *Sustainable development and tourism in a biosphere reserve: A case study of Lake Vänern Archipelago Biosphere Reserve, Sweden.* PhD dissertation. Karlstad: Faculty of Arts and Social Sciences, Human Geography, Karlstad University.

Kjellqvist, T., Rodela, R., & Lehtilä, K. (2020). Meeting the challenge of sustainable development: Analysing the knowledge used to establish Swedish biosphere reserves. In M. G. Reed & M. F. Price (Eds.), *UNESCO Biosphere Reserves: Supporting Biocultural Diversity, Sustainability and Society* (pp. 102–113). London & New York: Routledge.

Matsuda, H., Nakamura, S., & Sato, T. (2020). Transdisciplinary approaches for the reactivation of Japanese biosphere reserves. In M. G. Reed & M. F. Price (Eds.), *UNESCO Biosphere Reserves: Supporting Biocultural Diversity, Sustainability and Society* (pp. 190–200). London & New York: Routledge.

Onaindia, M., Herrero, C., Hernández, A, de Lucio, J. V., Pou, A., Barber, J., Rueda, T., Varela, B., Rodríguez, B. & Miguélez, A. et al. (2020). Co-creation of sustainable development knowledge in biosphere reserves. In M. G. Reed & M. F. Price (Eds.), *UNESCO Biosphere Reserves: Supporting Biocultural Diversity, Sustainability and Society,* 269–280. London & New York: Routledge.

24   *Eva Maria Jernsand et al.*

Pohl, C., Truffer, B., & Hirsch Hadorn, G. (2017). Addressing wicked problems through transdisciplinary research. In R. Frodeman, J. T. Klein, & R. C. D. S Pacheco (Eds.), *The Oxford Handbook of Interdisciplinarity* (pp. 319–331). Oxford: Oxford University Press.

Polk, M., & Kain, J.-H. (2015). Co-producing knowledge for sustainable urban futures. In M. Polk (Ed.), *Co-producing Knowledge for Sustainable Cities: Joining Forces for Change* (pp. 1–22). Abingdon & New York: Routledge.

Ranefjärd, N. (2018). Gästnattsrapport Västsverige (helårsrapport). *Turistrådet Västsverige.* www.vastsverige.com/contentassets/35f11e04ab244bcf9b64 80b264245333/inkvarteringsstatistik-helar-2018 – vastsverige.pdf

Ranefjärd, N. (2019). Gästnattsrapport Västsverige (helårsrapport). *Turistrådet Västsverige.* www.vastsverige.com/contentassets/ee5f8fac410846f18f71223ab932d614/ inkvarteringsstatistik-helar-2019 – turistradet-vastsverige.pdf

Ranefjärd, N. (2020). Gästnattsrapport Västsverige (helårsrapport). *Turistrådet Västsverige.* www.vastsverige.com/contentassets/a5e4a981607844b992a04c0d653cfcf7/ inkvarteringsstatisik-helar-2020.pdf

Reed, M. G., & Price, M. F. (2020a). Introducing UNESCO biosphere reserves. In M. G. Reed & M. F. Martin (Eds.), *UNESCO Biosphere Reserves: Supporting Biocultural Diversity, Sustainability and Society* (pp. 1–10). London & New York: Routledge.

Reed, M. G., & Price, M. F. (2020b). Unfinished business: The present and future contributions of biosphere reserves to sustainability science. In M. G. Reed & M. F. Price (Eds.), *UNESCO Biosphere Reserves: Supporting Biocultural Diversity, Sustainability and Society* (pp. 321–332). Abingdon & New York: Routledge.

Region Västra Götaland (2016). Handlingsprogram för hållbara maritima näringar Beslutad av: regionutvecklingsnämnden. https://tinyurl.se/4Eu.

Region Västra Götaland (n.d.). *Västerhavsveckan.* http://vasterhavsveckan.se/ the-west-coast-maritime-week/.

Rittel, H. W., & Webber, M. M. (1973). Dilemmas in a general theory of planning. *Policy Sciences*, 4(2), 155–169. https://doi.org/10.1007/BF01405730

Saarinen, J. (2013). Critical sustainability: Setting the limits to growth and responsibility in tourism. *Sustainability*, 6(1), 1–17.

Schianetz, K., Jones, T., Kavanagh, L., Walker, P. A., Lockington, D., & Wood, D. (2009). The practicalities of a learning tourism destination: A case study of the Ningaloo Coast. *International Journal of Tourism Research*, 11(6), 567–581. https://doi.org/10.1002/jtr.729

Scott, D., Hall, C. M., & Gössling, S. (2016). A review of the IPCC 5th Assessment and implications for tourism sector climate resilience and decarbonization. *Journal of Sustainable Tourism*, 24(1), 8–30. https://doi.org/10.1080/09669582.2015.1062021

Shaw, P., Shore, M., Bennett, E. H., & Reed, M. G. (2020). Perspectives on growth and change in Canada's 18 UNESCO biosphere reserves. In M. G. Reed & M. F. Price (Eds.), *UNESCO Biosphere Reserves: Supporting Biocultural Diversity, Sustainability and Society* (pp. 76–88). Abingdon & New York: Routledge.

Shoemaker, S. (1994). Segmenting the US travel market according to benefits realized. *Journal of Travel Research*, 32(3), 8–15. https://doi.org/10.1177/ 004728759403200303

Su, D. N., Johnson, L. W., & O'Mahony, B. (2018). Analysis of push and pull factors in food travel motivation. *Current Issues in Tourism*, 23(3), 1–15. https://doi.org/ 10.1080/13683500.2018.1553152

Těšitela, J., & Kušová, D. (2020). The more institutional models, the more challenges: Biosphere reserves in the Czech Republic. In M. G. Reed & M. F. Price (Eds.), *UNESCO Biosphere Reserves: Supporting Biocultural Diversity, Sustainability and Society* (pp. 125–134). Abingdon & New York: Routledge.

UN (2019). Summary of the SDG summit 2019. https://sustainabledevelopment. un.org/content/documents/25200SDG_Summary.pdf

UN (2021). *Satellite event: The European SDG summit 2021: For climate action and a just transition*. https://europa.eu/climate-pact/events/satellite-event-european-sdg-summit-2021-climate-action-just-transition_sv.

UNESCO (1996). *Biosphere Reserves: The Seville Strategy and the Statutory Framework of the World Network*. Paris: UNESCO. https://unesdoc.unesco.org/ ark:/48223/pf0000103849?posInSet=1&queryId=dad8e720-fb92-4464-b84c-5b991db9bc54.

UNESCO (2021a). *Man and the biosphere (MAB) programme*. https://en.unesco. org/mab.

UNESCO (2021b). *Biosphere reserves*. https://en.unesco.org/biosphere.

University of Gothenburg (n.d.). Ocean. www.gu.se/en/ocean

Volgger, M., Erschbamer, G., & Pechlaner, H. (2021). Destination design: New perspectives for tourism destination development. *Journal of Destination Marketing & Management*, 19. https://doi.org/10.1016/j.jdmm.2021.100561

Walk, H., Luthard, V., & Nöting, B. (2020). Participatory learning for transdisciplinary science in biosphere reserves. In M. G. Reed & M. F. Martin (Eds.), *UNESCO Biosphere Reserves: Supporting Biocultural Diversity, Sustainability and Society* (pp. 297–308). London and New York: Routledge.

WSP (2020). *Bohuskust. Utredning om förutsättningar för etablerandet av ett biosfärområde längs Bohusläns kustzon*. Gothenburg: WSP.

3 Science tourism

A conceptual development

Erik Lundberg, Maria Persson
and Eva Maria Jernsand

The systematic production of knowledge in universities, research centres and other organizations (such as hospitals, think tanks and firms) fulfils multiple purposes. Most commonly, we think of the production of theoretical insights explaining how the world works, or applied knowledge which can help organizations solve societal problems or develop new products (see Gibbons, 1994). However, as travel motives related to learning, personal development and transformative experiences are becoming more important (see chapter 1), science is also of interest for more direct tourism consumption through touristic experiences, attractions and destinations – science tourism.

Science tourism is defined as an activity in which individuals travel, outside of their home environment, "to learn about or participate in science" (Packer, 2015, p. 930), or more specifically, as tourism where "science, scientific knowledge, and/or engagement in scientific research" (Räikkönen et al., 2021, p. 2) is the core of tourists' motivation and experiences (Räikkönen et al., 2019; Räikkönen et al., 2021). Science tourism is most often depicted as a niche or special interest tourism within other forms of tourism, such as exploration and adventure tourism, cultural tourism, volunteer tourism, nature-based tourism, ecotourism or learning and educational tourism (Mao & Bourlon, 2011; Packer, 2015; Räikkönen et al., 2021). There is a limited scope of scholarly output focusing on science tourism (see Räikkönen et al., 2021). This is why there is a need for a conceptualization to guide further research efforts and public and private tourism actors.

Before going further, we need to separate science tourism from scientific tourism. The latter most often refers to researchers travelling for fieldwork, conferences or other scientific work (sometimes acting as tourists). This type of travel has been covered directly or indirectly in previous research (see Laarman & Perdue, 1989; Farrell & Runyan, 1991). However, in this chapter we explore science tourism as travel for leisure by (most often) non-scientists in which science and scientific work is the foundation of participants' travel

DOI: 10.4324/9781003293316-3

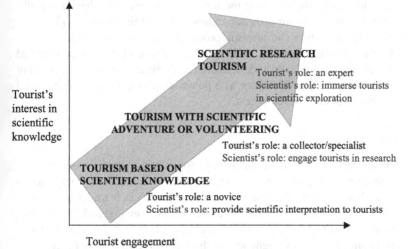

Tourist engagement

Figure 3.1 The framework of science tourism (Räikkönen et al., 2021), illustrating the relationship between tourists' interests in scientific knowledge and their engagement in scientific activities.

motivation and travel experiences. We also want to emphasize that science tourism covers multiple scientific areas, such as natural science, archaeology, technology and food studies, as well as history and art.

Previous research on science tourism focuses on defining and conceptualizing science tourism primarily from the perspective of the tourist, with regard, for example, to tourists' travel motivations and interest in different types of science tourism activities (Räikkönen et al., 2021; Bourlon & Torres, 2016). Building on this work, the objective of this chapter is to provide an extended conceptualization, including the tourist's perspective, but mainly considering scientists' (or scientific institutions') role in co-creating science tourism experiences (as demanded by, e.g., Räikkönen et al., 2021 and Higuchi & Yamanaka, 2017), and to what degree science tourism providers (e.g. museums, national parks, scientific institutions, tour guides) are embedded in the tourism industry. This last is important for several reasons, for example to reach new markets (outside the local region), to gain the ability to provide high-quality tourism experiences and, in general, for a higher level of professionalization.

In this chapter, we discuss science tourism providers' 1) level of embeddedness in science, 2) level of embeddedness in the tourism industry and (3) level of tourist immersion – that is, how the providers, through their activities, enable/enhance tourists' immersion and engagement in the activities. These three characteristics of science tourism will be exemplified with brief case studies in the form of vignettes. The chapter contributes theoretically to our growing understanding of the connection between scientific production and touristic production and lays out possible alleys of research going forward. It also contributes knowledge for current and future science tourism providers, as well as destination managers who want to gain insights into this sector as a potential vehicle for economic, social and environmental development.

Methods

The conceptual development of science tourism is primarily based on a literature review drawing on previous literature on science tourism (which is scarce but growing), but also on related fields such as learning and experiences. In order to illustrate the conceptual model (see Figure 3.2), vignettes are presented to briefly describe three different existing providers of science tourism activities. Vignettes are short narratives, stories or descriptions focusing on the research topic. Vignettes are flexible in form and give a snapshot of a relevant feature, in this case, to elaborate on a theoretical conceptualization by introducing particular aspects of fieldwork (Liburd et al., 2020; Heldbjerg & Liempd, 2018). In our case, the vignettes describe science tourism providers that have been part of our empirical context (West

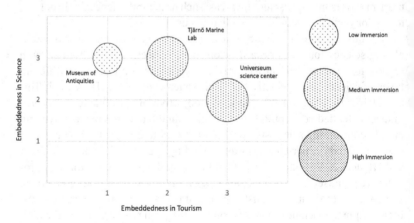

Note. 1 = low embeddedness, 2 = medium embeddedness, 3 = high embeddedness

Figure 3.2 The science tourism providers' embeddedness in the tourism industry (*x* axis) and science (*y* axis), and their activities in relation to tourist immersion (small to large circles).

Source: Authors' figure

Sweden) in the research project "Knowledge tourism as an attraction and resource," carried out from 2020 to 2022. The third vignette describes a research station that has been a central part of the research project, with several data collections during the course of the project (interviews, participant observation and action research activities), while the first two vignettes describe a museum of antiquities and a science centre that do not play a central role in the research project but serve as suitable illustrations of the conceptual model.

Literature review and conceptual development

Each section that follows is connected to the three characteristics of science tourism presented previously, followed by a conceptualization of science tourism from the perspective of a science tourism provider.

Science tourism providers' embeddedness in science

A science tourism provider can be analyzed based on how close to or how far they are situated from scientific knowledge production. This link, or embeddedness in science, has not been thoroughly problematized in previous science tourism research and Räikkönen et al. (2021) demand future research that highlights "the scientists' role in the value co-creation of tourism experiences" (p. 15). Their call focuses on tourists' demand for direct access to science communication, instead of professional tour guides or other sources of scientific knowledge. However, the embeddedness in science of a tourism initiative (e.g. scientists acting as guides or engaging tourists in research work, or a scientific institution that is providing the science tourism experience) would also influence the accuracy of the mediated scientific knowledge, its trustworthiness and ultimately the scientific quality of the experience.

Scientific mediation is "the interface between an audience and scientific knowledge" (Vialette et al., 2021, p. 4). Thus, the question of *who* the mediator is and *how* science is mediated in the science tourism setting determines the level of embeddedness in science. Who the mediator is, for example a scientist, a research centre or a professional guide, will influence both the content (how science is translated) and the delivery. How it is mediated refers both to the activities (e.g. guided tours or activities where tourists are involved in knowledge production) and the physical location of the mediation (e.g. a research centre, a museum or a hotel). If the distance (in terms of time and space) between the scientific knowledge (production) and its audience (i.e. the tourist) is great, then there is a risk that the audience will experience an incorrect, simplified or diluted version of the scientific knowledge. Thus, the science tourism provider's level of embeddedness in science will be analyzed on these terms and categorized as low, medium or high (see Figure 3.2).

Science tourism providers' embeddedness in the tourism industry

Even if a high level of embeddedness in science would facilitate the production of a high-quality science tourism experience, it is also necessary to consider the embeddedness of the science tourism provider in the tourism industry itself. The premise is that an actor with extensive experience of designing tourist experiences, with an extensive network in the tourism industry and knowledge about tourism demand would be able to provide a high-quality science tourism experience.

The tourism industry is fragmented (including transport, accommodation, attractions, activity providers, restaurateurs, retail, local governments, destination marketing and management organizations, etc.) and a key factor is collaboration across sectors in order to provide high-quality sustainable experiences (see Beritelli, 2011). This collaboration can be seen in local, regional and national tourism networks, of which some science tourism providers (with high embededdness) are part, while others (with low embeddedness) are outside. Being part of tourism networks could, according to van der Zee and Vanneste (2015), in their review of tourism network research, help improve the quality of tourism products and services, as well as improving sustainability work and competitiveness.

In terms of knowledge about the market and competence in designing tourist experiences, there is normally a difference between research institutions and, for example, museums or science centres. The latter two encounter tourists on a regular basis while the typical research institution does not. This means a science tourism provider is more or less embedded in the tourism industry through knowledge and experience of tourism (i.e. tourism competence).

Thus, in this chapter, the level of embeddedness in the tourism industry is analyzed based on collaboration and tourism competence and is categorized as low, medium or high embeddedness (see Figure 3.2).

Tourists' immersion and science tourism

From a tourist's perspective, previous studies show that there are several travel motivations driving science tourism demand. Excitement, adventure, enjoying nature, escape, relaxation and, most importantly, learning are motivations that can be identified (Bourlon & Torres, 2016; Räikkönen et al., 2021; West, 2008). These overlap with other core travel motivations of tourists, such as novelty seeking and escapism, found in more traditional travel motiva-tion studies, but also with more peripheral or special interest motivations, such as personal development (learning) and enjoying nature (see Pearce & Lee, 2005). It must be noted that previous research on science tourism travel motivations are predominantly carried out in a nature tourism context (thus the appearance of "enjoying nature" among the motivations listed). Sci-ence tourism could also take place in urban contexts (e.g. science centres and museums), at cultural heritage sites and beyond. For instance, if there is a connection to research activities, you may feel involved in an explora-tory adventure, while visiting historical sites can give a sense of closeness, of gaining access to a bygone era. The touristic context would probably modify travel motivations, although learning should be (and seems to be) at the core.

Räikkönen et al. (2021) provide a useful framework in their study on tourists' motivations and engagement at a Finnish nature-based science tourism attraction. They conceptualize three different types of science tour-ism experiences relating to the tourist's interest in scientific knowledge and engagement in the experience (see Figure 3.1). Based on, for instance, Trauer's (2006) categorization of special interest tourists' roles as novices, collectors, specialists and experts, the authors assume a linear increase in engagement, participation, knowledge and interest that can be translated into three different types of science tourism: 1) tourism based on scientific knowledge, 2) tourism involving scientific adventure or volunteering and 3) scientific research tourism. The first type (with the lowest level of engage-ment) is exemplified as typical guided tours where scientific knowledge is communicated to tourists. In the second type, tourists are participating in scientific work by, for example, going on a field excursion and making observations and/or collecting data. The third type, scientific research tour-ism, should be more immersive and include longer research experiences where tourists participate in fieldwork led by a researcher.

Based on the framework by Räikkönen et al. (2021), the current con-ceptualization will refer to three levels of tourist immersion (low, medium and high). It is particularly the level of immersion in the experience (with science) that is referred to, since deep engagement is essential for the pos-sibility of attaining transformative learning or transformational tourism (Walker & Moscardo, 2014; Reisinger, 2013). In the framework by Räik-könen et al. (2021) there is an assumption that the tourist takes on different roles (as a "novice," "collector/specialist" or "expert") based on skills. This is necessary in order to participate in higher-level science tourism, such as scientific research tourism. This is not considered in the current concep-tualization since it is assumed that a professional guide, service provider or researcher is an expert who can deliver an immersive, highly engaging science tourism experience. Furthermore, so-called tourist career ladders, whereby tourists achieve higher-level motives, consumption or, in this case, types of experiences, have been criticized for being too hierarchical and not depicting tourist behaviour accurately (Pearce & Lee, 2005).

Science tourism conceptualization

Based on the discussion in the preceding section, the three characteristics of science tourism providers can be illustrated in a matrix estimating the levels of embeddedness in tourism (x axis) and science (y axis) (see Figure 3.2). The providers in the upper right corners have the prerequisites to provide high-quality science tourism with close connections to both the tourism industry and the sources of scientific knowledge. They can be called *embedded* science tourism providers. In contrast, providers in the bottom left corner of the matrix are *detached* science tourism providers with low embeddedness in both science and tourism.

However, it is also important to understand the level of tourist engagement, which could help us understand whether they provide more immersive and possibly transformative experiences (Walker & Moscardo, 2014; Reisinger, 2013). The level of tourist immersion is illustrated by the three different-sized circles, depicting low, medium and high immersion (see Figure 3.2). It is important to note that tourism demand for high-engagement experiences is not always greater (see Räikkönen et al., 2021). Service providers need to adapt their offered experiences depending on context and tourists' travel motivations. However, higher levels of embeddedness in tourism and science facilitate the adaption and delivery of high-quality experiences on all immersion levels.

It is important to highlight that the ultimate goal for all science tourism providers cannot (and should not) be in the far-right corner of the matrix (i.e. embedded science providers), providing highly immersive experiences. This must be a strategic choice for individual providers. However, the conceptualization might serve as a tool to describe and analyze a provider's current market position and thus help in strategy development, in changing position or in maintaining the current position.

The science tourism providers and their activities that are described in the vignettes have been plotted in the matrix.

Vignettes

The following three examples of science tourism providers, a university-run museum, a science centre and a university research station, illustrate different levels of embeddedness in science and tourism, and their activities in relation to tourist immersion. In addition to illustrating the conceptualization (Figure 3.2), the examples also provide insights into possible strategies for science tourism providers on how to increase embeddedness and immersion. Each vignette briefly describes the science tourism provider and its touristic activities, and finishes with suggested levels of embeddedness and engagement.

Vignette 1: Museum of Antiquities, a museum within the Faculty of Humanities, University of Gothenburg

Inside the entrance to the Faculty of Humanities at University of Gothenburg, Sweden, a statue of Aphrodite greets the visitor, pointing toward the Museum of Antiquities. The museum is part of the Department of Historical Studies and is run by the section for Classical Archaeology and Ancient History. In the museum, you can find collections of original artefacts from the classical Mediterranean cultures, including pottery, Roman coins and Latin funerary inscriptions. The collections have a special focus on Greece, Italy and Cyprus. The original artefacts are in museum cases, their displays divided into different geographical areas. There are also replicas of well-known artefacts and statues, such as busts of emperors and philosophers. The museum first opened in 1984 and the majority of collections originate from archaeological projects carried out by Swedish archaeologists, mostly on Cyprus.

The museum is used in university education, foremost in courses in Classical Archaeology and Ancient History. Several different learning activities take place in the museum, such as lectures, drawing assignments and artefact documentation. The museum is not open to the public on a regular basis. For the time being it is open only for pre-booked visits and on special occasions.

When taking a guided tour of the Museum of Antiquities, the visitor is shown around the collections by a researcher in Classical Archaeology and Ancient History. There are no trained guides and the information that there is a museum here cannot be found in public brochures or websites that visitors to Gothenburg normally come into contact with. Many different themes can be approached with a starting point in the collections. One example is the large collection of Roman coins, showing the role of coins as a medium of mass communication in Roman society. The museum also has Roman grave inscriptions, from both free and enslaved persons, giving important information about these large and subaltern groups of people in Roman society. The participant can experience either a general tour of the collections and of Mediterranean archaeology, or a specific subject can be approached by the researcher doing the tour.

Embeddedness and immersion model

The museum has a low level of embeddedness in the tourism industry (equivalent to level 1 in Figure 3.2), since it is not currently open to the public on a regular basis and neither the scientists who lead the tours nor the museum are part of tourist networks. However, the museum has a high level of embeddedness in science (level 3 in Figure 3.2), being closely involved with research, located at the university campus and with tours given by researchers. Furthermore, the opportunity for visitors to become immersed in activities at the Museum of Antiquities is low, as depicted in Figure 3.1 by Räikkönen et al. (2021) and by the small circle of engagement (size 1) in Figure 3.2. The guided tours merely include scientists' provision of scientific interpretation to visitors, without much interaction unless questions are asked.

Vignette 2: Universeum, a national science centre focusing on experience-based learning

A phenomenon that can be included in the framework of science tourism is so-called science centres. They are visitor attractions with a focus on learning linked to science and technology. The number of science centres is increasing worldwide and today there are over 3,000 (Swedish Science Centres, n.d.). What they all have in common is that they work to stimulate interest in science, technology and innovation. Usually their target groups are children and young people. Science centres are often regarded as an official complement to school lessons in science and technology.

Science centres are also important tourist destinations. Sweden's largest science centre, Universeum, in Gothenburg, has half a million visitors per year. Its business is rooted in the mindset that increased knowledge leads to increased sustainability. Its learning methodology focuses on experiential learning, where the visitor has the opportunity to learn about and experience contexts such as space, the rainforest and the sea, among other things. This can be experienced through guided tours, by watching shows or by taking an active part in experiments of different kinds.

Both Chalmers University of Technology and the University of Gothenburg are founders of Universeum; it is based on science and developed in collaboration with academia (Universeum, n.d.) Recently, a professorship was established that connects pedagogical research with technology and digitization at Universeum. The purpose is to promote learning at Universeum and conduct research on data visualization and learning. The establishment of the professorship means a strengthened collaboration between Universeum and the University of Gothenburg, and also means that the science centre will be a place for applied research (University of Gothenburg, n.d.a; Universeum, n.d).

The degree of research affiliation at different science centres varies. They are all closely linked to business and innovation. However, research is not conducted at science centres in general, which means that one of the parameters of science tourism is not met. However, they are a very important contact point between science, children and young people, business and tourism.

Embeddedness and immersion model

Universeum has a high level of embeddedness in tourism, as an integral part of local and regional tourism networks with visitor numbers of half a million per year. However, although the science centre has strong affiliations and cooperation with research and its activities are based on scientific knowledge, its embeddedness in research is here considered medium (level 2) since research is not conducted there and researchers are not heavily involved in its scientific mediation. Universeum's focus on experience-based learning, including, for example, the opportunity for the visitor to take an active part in experiments, generates a medium level of tourist immersion (circle size 2) in the model.

Vignette 3: Tjärnö Marine Laboratory, a university laboratory open to the public

Tjärnö Marine Laboratory is a research station for marine university education and research in the marine sciences. It is part of the Marine Infrastructure at the University of Gothenburg and hosts students and researchers from Sweden and abroad. The research station is located on the Swedish west coast, in the country's most species-rich marine area – the Kosterhavet National Park.

The public is welcome to visit Tjärnö Marine Laboratory and there is a well-developed infrastructure to facilitate these visits. The laboratory is located in a popular tourism area and most of the activities offered take place during vacation periods, although pre-booked visits are available all year round (University of Gothenburg, n.d.b).

The activities offered consist of guided tours of the facilities, beach excursions, summer camps for children and research vessel excursions. Most activities are linked to current and ongoing research and are presented by marine biologists and researchers at the station. The research station also has the most species-rich aquarium in Sweden. The Tjärnö aquarium is the centre point of the public visits to the research station. It is open daily during the summer vacation period and a visit incorporates an introduction, a movie, entrance to the aquarium hall and the opportunity to look at small living organisms in stereomicroscope (University of Gothenburg, n.d.b).

Figure 3.3 Research-led boat excursion, Tjärnö Marine Laboratory.

Photo: Maria Persson

As already mentioned, the visitor to Tjärnö Marine Laboratory has the opportunity to go on a research vessel trip. The tour, called "Diversity of the Sea," takes the participant out on the waters near the research station where several research-affiliated activities take place. With assistance from the participants, measurements of the water, such as of salinity and seawater transparency, are performed. One of the main activities onboard is to take samples from the bottom of the sea, where the dredge brings algae and animals from the seabed up onto deck. On the observation platform, the visitors go through the collected species together with the researcher/guide, who informs them about the findings. This is followed up back at the laboratory facilities where the participants can study the algae and animals in stereomicroscope, also a part of the tour activity. The tour takes 2.5 hours and is available for pre-booked visits. The guide on these excursions is most often a researcher in marine sciences and on some occasions non-research staff at the station (Figure 3.3).

Embeddedness and immersion model

Tjärnö Marine Laboratory has a programme and activities that are clearly directed at tourists, and a large number of visitors. They also collaborate with local tourism actors, although neither visitor numbers nor levels of collaboration are high in comparison with Universeum. Therefore, Tjärnö Marine Laboratory corresponds to a medium level of tourism embeddedness (2) in the model (Figure 3.2). However, as a research station, it has a high level of embeddedness in science (level 3). Research is conducted at the station, the tourist activities are closely connected to research and many of the tourist activities are organized by researchers. Lastly, Tjärnö Marine Laboratory has a medium level of tourist engagement, offering scientific adventures such as beach excursions and research vessel tours (level 2 in Figure 3.2).

Concluding discussion

This chapter has provided a conceptualization of science tourism focusing on the science tourism provider. In order to deliver high-quality science tourism experiences, it is important to consider science tourism providers' embeddedness in the tourism industry and in science. Furthermore, it is vital to understand tourists' travel motivations and interest in science tourism in order to deliver experiences that meet tourists' willingness to engage, from more passive participation (e.g. guided tours) to immersive scientific research tourism (see Räikkönen et al., 2021).

The conceptual model of embeddedness and immersion in science tourism (Figure 3.2) provides an analytical lens for both researchers and practitioners in science tourism. For the latter, it gives providers the possibility to evaluate strategic decisions on different levels in order to become more embedded as science tourism providers, to maintain their current positions or to be more detached. Since tourists show an increasing interest in seeking personal development on vacation and engaging in transformational experiences, the model makes for an important contribution. Service providers that want to increase their embeddedness in tourism should seek out local, regional and national tourism networks, which are often coordinated by destination marketing or management organizations (DMOs). These networks have substantial experience of packaging and marketing tourist experiences and may be able to connect the provider with other suitable tourist actors. To increase embeddedness in science can be a challenge, but a first step could be to find common goals where the service provider and a research institution (or individual researchers) could meet, for example to devise joint projects to develop tourist experiences while also conducting research.

Further research on science tourism should apply the conceptual model empirically by conducting case studies on science tourism providers with different levels of embeddedness. This would help us to understand challenges and opportunities for science tourism actors with different prerequisites. These case studies should, preferably, cover multiple types of tourism, going beyond nature-based science tourism to include cultural heritage tourism, urban tourism or special interest tourism, such as sport and event tourism. The extension into varying settings should also include studies of tourists' motivations for participating in science tourism in order to build on previous research by Räikönnen et al. (2021) and Bourlon and Torres (2016).

References

Beritelli, P. (2011). Cooperation among prominent actors in a tourist destination. *Annals of Tourism Research*, 38(2), 607–629. https://doi.org/10.1016/j.annals.2010.11.015

Bourlon, F., & Torres, R. (2016). *Scientific tourism, a tool for tourism development in Patagonia*. https://labexitem. hypotheses.org/177

Farrell, B. H., & Runyan, D. (1991). Ecology and tourism. *Annals of Tourism Research*, 18(1), 26–40. https://doi.org/10.1016/0160-7383(91)90037-C

Gibbons, M. (Ed.) (1994). *The New Production of Knowledge: The Dynamics of Science and Research in Contemporary Societies*. London: Sage.

Heldbjerg, G., & Liempd, D. V. (2018). Vignettes in critical theory investigations. In P. V. Freytag & L. Young (Eds.), *Collaborative Research Design: Working with Industry for Meaningful Findings* (pp. 313–340). Springer. https://link.springer.com/chapter/10.1007/978-981-10-5008-4_13

Higuchi, Y., & Yamanaka, Y. (2017). Knowledge sharing between academic researchers and tourism practitioners: A Japanese study of the practical value of embeddedness, trust and co-creation. *Journal of Sustainable Tourism*, 25(10), 1456–1473. http://dx.doi.org/10.1080/09669582.2017.1288733

Laarman, J. G., & Perdue, R. R. (1989). Science tourism in Costa Rica. *Annals of Tourism Research*, 16(2), 205–215. https://doi.org/10.1016/0160-7383(89)90068-6

Liburd, J., Duedahl, E., & Heape, C. (2020). Co-designing tourism for sustainable development, *Journal of Sustainable Tourism*. https://doi.org/10.1080/09669582.2020.1839473

Mao, P., & Bourlon, F. (2011). Le tourisme scientifique: un essai de définition. *Téoros: Revue de recherche en tourisme*, 30(2), 94–104. https://doi.org/10.7202/1012246ar

Packer, J. (2015). Science tourism. In R. Gunstone (Ed.), *Encyclopedia of Science Education* (pp. 930–932). Dordrecht: Springer. https://doi.org/10.1007/978-94-007-2150-0

Pearce, P. L., & Lee, U.-I. (2005). Developing the travel career approach to tourist motivation. *Journal of Travel Research*, 43(3), 226–237. https://doi.org/10.1177%2F0047287504272020

Räikkönen, J., Grénman, M., Rouhiainen, H., Honkanen, A., & Sääksjärvi. I. E. (2021). Conceptualizing nature-based science tourism: A case study of Seili Island, Finland. *Journal of Sustainable Tourism*. https://doi.org/10.1080/09669582.2021.1948553

Räikkönen, J., Rouhiainen, H., Grénman, M., & Sääksjärvi, I. E. (2019). Advancing environmental sustainability through nature-based science tourism: The potential of universities. *Finnish Journal of Tourism Research*, 15(1), 67–87. https://doi.org/10.33351/mt.79852

Reisinger, Y. (Ed.). (2013). *Transformational Tourism: Tourist Perspectives*. Wallingford: CABI. http://dx.doi.org/10.1079/9781780642093.0000

Swedish Science Centres (n.d.). *Science centers i världen*. https://fssc.se/science-centers-i-varlden/.

Trauer, B. (2006). Conceptualizing special interest tourism – Frameworks for analysis. *Tourism Management*, 27(2), 183–200. https://doi.org/10.1016/j.tourman.2004.10.004

Universeum (n.d.). www.universeum.se/en/.

University of Gothenburg (n.d.-a). *New professor to work with data visualisation at Universeum*. www.gu.se/en/news/new-professor-to-work-with-data-visualisation-at-universeum.

University of Gothenburg (n.d.-b). Tjärnö marine laboratory. *Schools and the Public*. www.gu.se/en/tjarno/schools-and-the-public.

van der Zee, E., & Vanneste, D. (2015). Tourism networks unravelled: A review of the literature on networks in tourism management studies. *Tourism Management Perspectives*, 15, 46–56. https://doi.org/10.1016/j.tmp.2015.03.006

Vialette, Y., Mao, P., & Bourlon, F. (2021). Scientific tourism in the French alps: A laboratory for scientific mediation and research. *Journal of Alpine Research | Revue de géographie alpine*, 109(2). https://doi.org/10.4000/rga.9189

Walker, K., & Moscardo, G. (2014). Encouraging sustainability beyond the tourist experience: Ecotourism, interpretation and values. *Journal of Sustainable Tourism*, 22(8), 1175–1196. https://doi.org/10.1080/09669582.2014.918134

West, P. (2008). Tourism as science and science as tourism. *Current Anthropology*, 49(4), 597–626. https://doi.org/10.1086/586737

4 Learning on guided tours

Historical perspectives

Malin Zillinger and Jan-Henrik Nilsson

Tourism offers manifold opportunities for learning. Tourists on the move learn generic skills such as social awareness, problem solving and adaptability. Tourists can also learn about place-specific matters such as landscape development, architectural history or cultural milieus. Among others, Broomhall et al. (2010) underline the potential of tourism for lifelong learning outside of formal education. One way for tourists to be exposed to place-specific information is through a guided tour. Guided tours have proven to be resilient in their structure, as they have adapted to the changing needs of tourists (Widtfeldt Meged & Zillinger, 2018). They have adapted to new sorts of demand, in line with the ever-changing facets of tourism and of people's aspiration for learning. The role of the tour guide is multifaceted, but their main role is the communication of place-specific information (Weiler & Black, 2015).

We usually do not draw on dictionaries in research, but in this chapter, we include the 1933 *Oxford English Dictionary* definition of guides (p. iv, 491, cited from Cohen, 1985) because we think the description is peculiar from today's point of view. According to the dictionary, a guide is someone showing the way to travellers "in a strange country." With today's identity as cosmopolitans who have travelled the world, we react to the adjective "strange," although people may still consider unfamiliar places as strange: places they do not understand and need help to interpret. This small excerpt from an almost 100-year-old dictionary helps us understand that the role of guides has changed through the years. Relating this approach to the acquisition of knowledge, this chapter aims to discover the different roles that guides have had, and to explore how such roles have contributed to tourists' learning. We do so by building our argumentation on two theoretical frameworks: Cohen's (1985) categorization of the tourist guide and Falk et al.'s (2012) conceptual considerations on learning during travel. Together, these approaches contribute to our understanding of tourists' learning processes in guided tours.

DOI: 10.4324/9781003293316-4

Cohen (1985) places the origins of the modern guide in the time of the Grand Tour during the 17th and 18th centuries. One can argue that the Grand Tour is nothing but an answer to the aristocracy's request for more knowledge. Basic to Cohen (1985) is his recognition of development over time, where guide types are adapting to altered demands. In Cohen's categorization, tourist guides work either in a leadership or in a mediatory sphere, and attention is paid to how guiding relates to situations outside the group, or inside (see Table 4.1). The development over time goes from the *original guide*, via the *animator*, the *tour leader*, to the *professional guide*. In a nutshell, development goes from leadership with attention outside the group, to mediation with attention inside the group. However, in this chapter we will argue that these guide roles are present side by side in most guiding, and that there is no plain chronological development. Note also that Cohen published his seminal paper in 1985, years before the advent of innovations like the internet, platform industries or smartphones. This has consequences for our own analysis of guides in this book chapter.

Guides belong to different spheres. The original guide and the animator belong to the *leadership sphere*, which is split into instrumental, outward-directed and social, inward-directed leadership. The original guide is understood as being in an instrumental leadership sphere, while the animator belongs to the social range. The tour leader and professional guide both belong to the *mediatory sphere*, and are understood as interactional (tour leader) or communicative (professional guide).

The *original guide* can be likened to a pathfinder for explorers in unknown territory. They know how to navigate, have access to maps and to connoisseurs of the terrain and have social access to "back regions" (MacCannell, 1973, p. 597). This type of guide had a challenging task due to travellers' non-existent knowledge and experience of the region's geography and

Table 4.1 Tour guide roles. Based on Cohen (1985)

	Attention outside the group	Attention inside the group
Leadership sphere	Original guide Navigation Access to back regions Control and safety	Animator Tension management Integration Morale Marginally: animation
Mediatory sphere	Tour leader Representation Organization of service Communication	Professional guide Selection Information Interpretation Fabrication

people. Their control made the journey safe and efficient, paving the way for survival in challenging lands. Their knowledge came primarily from personal experience, and included geographical and social skills that they could share. These were important attributes when travellers could not easily ask for the right way, or when it was dangerous to talk to unknown people (Rotberg, 1970). The importance of pathfinders is exemplified in the expeditions through *terra incognita*, be it Carl Linnaeus's journeys to Lapland or Alexander von Humboldt's journeys to South America.

The *animator* primarily takes care of tension management in the group for integration and for good morale. The emphasis of this role is not on protection, but rather on inducement: the animator encourages the tourists to participate in the often hedonistic touristic facilities that are offered. In this way, the role of the animator is predominantly social. As a side note, Cohen (1985) mentions such duties as a compensation for inferior competence.

The *tour leader* acts as a middleman between the local population and travel group; thus, the focus is on interaction. This includes the integration of the group into the setting visited; the guide can open social doors for the visitors. It also includes the insulation of the group from the setting. In addition, tour leaders attend to representation as well as to the organization of services along the way.

The *professional guide*, Cohen's last guide type along his line of development, is concerned with the selection of attractions and services, and with information dissemination and interpretation. The focus is very much on communication between the place and its attractions, and the visitors. Professional guides thus act as teachers and instructors, and mediate possible cultural gaps between travellers and locals. They are usually well-educated outsiders capable of informal socialization. While original guides operate in the periphery of the tourism system, producing new attractions through their own work, professional guides contribute to the reproduction of attractions.

The second conceptualization in our study is based on Falk et al. (2012), who categorize learning in travel contexts. The authors state that learning has long been viewed negatively in popular culture. But today, learning is increasingly discovered as a positive experience that contributes to personal rewards. Tourists increasingly search for experiences that lead to an immersion in activities, and in the spaces around them. This can be a core motivational force, or can happen unintentionally, while doing other things. Much learning takes place outside of classroom environments. One advantage of this type of learning is the relationship between new information, place and emotional recognition. It has the potential to make long-lasting changes in both thoughts and actions. Falk et al. build their framework on the work of

Table 4.2 Conceptualization of learning in travel situations. Based on Falk et al. (2012)

	Active learning	Passive learning
Episteme: theoretical knowledge	Search for knowledge, e.g. learning about place and its history	Serendipitous (unexpected) acquisition of knowledge, e.g. hearing others talk about a place
Techne: practical skills	Aim to master a task, e.g. kayaking	Incidental development of skills, e.g. ability to adapt to new places
Phronesis: practical knowledge	Pursuit of a valued and abstract knowledge, e.g. learning about heritage	Accumulating life experience, e.g. cultural awareness

Aristotle, who claimed that knowledge is related to three different kinds of competencies (see Table 4.2).

Episteme is theoretical knowledge that is systematic and universal across contexts. For example, it can consist of knowledge about sites or settings. It can be acquired spontaneously or intentionally. *Techne* refers to practical skills and routines. Tourists can incidentally develop skills, or actively learn to master them. *Phronesis* is about practical wisdom, where experiential knowledge is related to specific contexts. It appears as passively accumulated life experience, or as conscious learning about behaviours and perspectives. It is about acting in the right way, and for the right reasons, including reflexivity about one's actions (Saugstad, 2005). Both Aristotle and Cohen may help us to understand what guiding looks like, and to identify different kinds of learning that appear on tours. However, while we know that learning occurs during guiding, there has been no systematic approach yet related to guide roles and learning conceptualization on guided tours.

In order to integrate Cohen (1985) and Falk et al. (2012) with guided tours, we work in four chronological steps. These are 1) guiding and the Grand Tour, 2) tourism in industrial Europe, 3) post-war mass tourism and 4) tourism in the digital age. During this journey in time, we aim to show through our examples that experiential and transformative learning have been closely related to one another over time. Technologies and contexts have changed, but some basic performative elements remain. Empirically, this chapter is based on tourism literature describing tourism development and guiding. The section on the digital age largely builds on empirical data published by Nilsson and Zillinger (2020). In extension to this, the webpages of guiding organizations are used to empirically underline selected arguments.

Guiding and the Grand Tour

Grand Tours commenced in the 17th century, but had their peak in the period 1760–1790, prior to the French Revolution. Grand Tours were in essence educational tours, often lasting for years. The educational character was emphasized by the presence of tutors or mentors (both terms are used) who accompanied the young men on the tour. The travellers were known as "tourists" and came from the upper classes of Northern Europe, mainly from Great Britain. Popular destinations were Paris, Rome, Florence and Naples, while university towns like Utrecht and capital cities such as Potsdam and Dresden attracted the more serious travellers (Cederberg, 2015). This means that there is no sharp division between the Grand Tours and academic peregrinations made by students and scholars. However, the wealthy tourists have come to represent Grand Tour travelling.

The purpose of these tours was to turn young boys into men of the world and the ruling elite – it was a social asset to be well travelled. The men needed skills in language, philosophy and politics, and knowledge of foreign cultures, especially the sophisticated continental manners. It was important to travel in a grand style, bringing large amounts of luggage and staff; there was a clear social connection between travel and consumption (Zuelow, 2016). Above all, aristocrats were expected to spend money matching their rank and fortune. Besides conspicuous consumption, this included buying extensive amounts of souvenirs to bring home. Many British collections of arts and antiquities were brought home from Grand Tours, and became material displays of their owners' social standing. Seen in this perspective, Grand Tours offered more than straightforward knowledge of "strange" places. Active learning of theoretical knowledge or practical skills was not the primary focus. Instead, the young tourists learnt a lot along the way, through the guidance of their tutors during these encounters. Emphasis was on practical knowledge, *phronesis*. Grand Tours can therefore be viewed as the process of becoming a gentleman, in which practical knowledge was embodied in a "consumable expression of refinement" (Zuelow, 2016, p. 22).

The Grand Tours were dependent on a system that offered structured skills and knowledge. The system consisted of mobile guides and immobile, aristocratic networks. The aristocrats welcomed their travelling noble guests in their homes. This upper-class network had a guiding function in explaining the social structures of the place, its history and architecture. Aristocrats gave travellers access to members of their private networks. These kinds of networks were of course not available to travellers outside the nobility. As the social structure of tourists came to include people from more bourgeois backgrounds, more people had to rely on commercial functions like guesthouses and local guides. Despite other changes, tutors accompanied the young men on their journeys (Brodsky-Porges, 1981) and acted as private teachers who cared for a few noblemen at a time. This included access to places and people, and explanations of structures and situations. Eighteenth-century travel was too difficult and dangerous to be left for the inexperienced tourists to manage alone. Guides' services included geographical knowledge and a high level of control, which made the journey both safer and more efficient.

Tutors combined their roles of pathfinders and organizers with that of educators, who guided their students to significant attractions. If well connected, they could also introduce the noblemen to important people. The quality of the tutors seems to have differed a lot, though. The famous historian of the Roman Empire Edward Gibbon had a tutor who introduced him to a broad range of places, fields of study, and people. James Boswell, a young Scotsman from a bourgeois background, paid visits to both Rousseau and Voltaire during his Grand Tour in the years 1763–1766 (Cederberg, 2015). In other cases, it was rather difficult to find people with the proper skills. Those who were available often had difficulties finding a career in their country of origin; however, they still needed some formal education to take on the task. According to Zuelow (2016, p. 25), most tutors were "untalented and inattentive" writers, academics or clergymen.

The tutors were also responsible for keeping their students away from all sorts of vice and trouble – inevitable consequences of sending young men abroad on their own. In the wider literature, there are plenty of examples of how they failed in this field of education, sometimes because they were bad examples themselves. In Italy, British tourists established a reputation for bad behaviour. A contemporary, Dr. Samuel Johnson, made the following comment on the issue: "If a young man is wild, and must run after women and bad company, it is better this should be done abroad" (cited in Zuelow, 2016, p. 28). It seems that "the tourist condition" has always been related to norm-breaking behaviour. This example shows that learning in tourism does not always work as expected. Nevertheless, the young 18th-century tourist did most likely accumulate much practical knowledge along the way, in understanding "strange" cultures and in coping with unknown and possibly unpleasant situations.

Tourism in industrial Europe

The role of tour guides changed in the middle of the 19th century when public transport was introduced. Steam ships and railways increased the speed and predictability of travel, which became less dependent on natural elements and instead relied on predetermined timetables. Increased passenger capacities and timetables enabled the organization of guided tours for larger ·

groups, following a detailed itinerary. This also meant that large groups of people received the same information. With rising degrees of organization, guides' roles changed and they became tour leaders. Following detailed itineraries, the guide's primary tasks were to hold the group together, to look after their guests and to make sure the group left and arrived on time (Hannavy, 2012). At the same time, they were expected to provide knowledge. In such circumstances, management tends to come first. If the practical aspects of travel do not work, the role of the professional guide cannot be performed.

This birth of modern mass tourism is associated with Thomas Cook, a preacher and printer from the English Midlands, who built his business model on economies of scale. Cook´s commercial breakthrough came with the 1851 London World Exhibition, an event that attracted millions of visitors largely travelling by public transport (Swinglehurst, 1982). At the beginning, Cook's tours mainly took place within Great Britain, but they gradually reached more international destinations. They were organizationally simple, and consisted of a return ticket and sometimes accommodations. Guiding was included, comprising group escorts and place interpretation. The invention of the package tour called for guides who understood the attractions visited, and who were able to explain them to a wider public. Through guiding, tourists learnt about attractions and their histories; they incidentally adapted to new places, and they accumulated life experience of travelling in a group in "strange" places (*phronesis*). The latter could be interpreted as a form of achievement that contributed to social advancement.

International guided tours catered to a resourceful clientele, mainly belonging to the upper middle class. Education and learning were ways of distancing the new middle classes from the leisured aristocracy of the past. The bourgeois culture of learning represented a culture of achievement (Hobsbawm, 1981). Learning became an aim of its own, including its representational value for social positioning. Hence, travel became serious. Now that status was included, it was essential to visit the right places and to see the right things. Guides were needed, as they made a selection. The corresponding genre of guidebooks played an important role in instructing tourists about culturally significant attractions, sometimes very ambitiously. For example, Baedeker (1878) spent 56 pages solely on the collections at the Louvre, Paris. Guidebooks thereby came to work as cultural canons. Modern means of transport and printed media such as guidebooks made travelling accessible to a wider audience in terms of both affordability and capability. In guidebooks, one could learn the art of travelling on one's own, from the confines of one's armchair.

With longer travel distances, people needed leisure, together with economic and cultural capital, to enjoy a journey abroad. According to the

British historian Eric Hobsbawm (1981, p. 281), a six-week round trip in western Europe cost £85 in the 1870s, a sum comparable to a worker's yearly earnings. Furthermore, professionals like lawyers, priests, teachers and doctors did not have unlimited means or leisure time. They demanded journeys that were rich in experiences, reasonably short and reasonably cheap. The argument of rationality became apparent. If one wants to maximize opportunities for positive experiences, learning and interpersonal relationships, guides can be of help. If time is limited, the guide can select "what ought to be seen" (Koshar, 1998, p. 323) by describing, clarifying and explaining phenomena on route. Such needs are new, and related to the new class of travellers: the middle class. Aristocrats, as described, had almost all the time in the world, as they were not dependent on paid work for their living.

One can also pay attention to the gendered aspects of learning on guided tours. In the late 19th century, women made up a large proportion of the participants in guided tours (Nilsson, 2016). This contrasts with previous periods when travellers, with few exceptions, were male. The format of packaged tours and the associated presence of guides provided predictability and a sense of safety. This made it socially acceptable for middle-class women to travel. Such a development shows the social importance of guiding. In other words, the effect of guides and guided tours is not restricted to the selection of places and attractions and to the information they disseminate, but also allows more people from diverse social backgrounds to participate in spatial mobility. However, most working-class people were unable to travel until paid vacations were introduced.

In Sweden, the Swedish Tourist Association (STF) organized the first group guided tours in the 1890s. STF's motto is "Know your country" (*Känn ditt land*) and the organization aims to teach Swedes about their country's nature, geography and history. STF still has the same purpose and motto today. Guided tours mainly took place in the Swedish mountain ranges, for hiking in summer and skiing in winter (von Seth, 2008). The participants came from the educated middle class, which is no surprise. They travelled with sufficient knowledge of nature, and aimed to explore new leisure spaces in the mountains. With rapid changes in weather and long distances between the mountain shelters, mountain areas could be dangerous. The qualities of the guides were therefore a combination of practical comprehension and of theoretical knowledge about the surrounding landscape. The former was particularly important in unknown and possibly dangerous territory. Guides brought leadership and mediatory competences, and their qualities were actually a mix of all four of Cohen's guide types.

Subsequently, the labour movement organized guided tours, just as similar organizations in other countries had done before. The Workers' Study

Organization (ABF) was a leading actor, driven by strong ideological standpoints. In 1937, one year before the introduction of two weeks' paid vacation, the labour movement started its own travel agency, RESO. Its aim was to offer both recreation and education to its members (Gråbacke, 2008). RESO's first major undertaking was tours to the World Exhibition in Paris in 1937. It was such a success that it was challenging to find enough educated guides. Students with labour sympathies were enrolled as supplements (von Seth, 2008). The role of these guides was similar to that of the tutors on the Grand Tours. They had knowledge of languages, history and foreign cultures, as well as of the organization of travel. If talented, they could also inspire the guests' own learning by highlighting interesting attractions along the way. In this case, learning had a clear purpose in inspiring practical knowledge. For this to occur, guides needed to perform numerous roles: navigators, organizers and sources of information.

World War II put an end to most leisure travel, except domestic travel, preferably by bicycle. After the war, travel slowly came back. At the beginning, the educational aspects of travel were prominent. Guided tours aimed at widening participants' horizons, often in a political context (Gråbacke, 2008). This is an interesting example of experience-based learning aimed at self-improvement and social advancement. Participants in guided tours were supposed to learn about the places they visited, not just to spend time in hedonistic pursuits. Tours often included visits to selected workplaces, with the intention of learning about working conditions in other areas. Such dissemination of skills was often provided by workers themselves – they were the real specialists. RESO was initially influenced by a strong tradition of self-education in the Swedish labour movement, including visits to libraries and evening classes. The labour movement wanted to lift its members to the same level of education as the middle classes. Many prominent social democratic politicians, such as the wartime prime minister Per Albin Hansson, followed such an informal educational career.

Post-war mass tourism

There was a strong rise in tourism in the early post-war period. Many people were curious about new places and had the ability to travel. Means of transport developed quickly, and made different kinds of learning environments possible, including those taking place while travelling. As guided tours were planned and performed to meet various demands, they became more diverse in character. The market increased, and more people became interested in travel for travel's sake, and not only as a form of self-education. Many tourists learnt how to travel internationally, first in groups and then on their own. Such a development demands an increasing variety of guiding practices, and requires different sorts of knowledge to be transmitted. In fact, the art of guiding is also dependent on the development of vehicles and the spaces created by them.

In the Nordic countries, coach buses dominated international tourism in the 1940s and 1950s. Aviation was expensive and highly regulated. The cost structure for coaches was reasonably low, which resulted in low entry barriers (Nilsson, 2012). Long-distance coach rides require regular stops along the way. Therefore, sightseeing became a standard part of the journey. Guiding takes place in the coach itself, which has specific qualities that resemble a classroom. There are normally between 25 and 50 people aboard, making it a cohesive group. The guide is equipped with a microphone, and easily points out attractions through the windows. Typically, there is one stop before and one stop after lunch. The guiding schedule and content are adapted to logistic conditions on the tour, and to time limits related to the distance covered during the day. The material structure of the vehicle made it entirely appropriate for tours that had their roots in popular education. Sitting in the guide seat of the coach, the guide can concentrate on her role as a professional guide. The time available is sufficient for rather extensive lectures. In the authors' experience, the practical role of the tour leader (see Cohen, 1985) is often shared between the guide and the bus driver. For example, the driver may be responsible for luggage while the guide manages check-ins at hotels. For guiding to be successful, many complementary tasks need to be orchestrated.

When charter tours by air were introduced, the final destination became the main reason for travelling, since there were no stops along the way – apart from stopovers at airports. Hence, the journey transformed into mere transport. Guiding is not possible aboard an aircraft, apart from the pilot's brief comments on landmarks and cities seen during flight. When jets were introduced, visibility was reduced to a minimum. The Swedish historian Thomas Kaiserfeld (2010) suggests that the lack of stops on journeys from Scandinavia to the Mediterranean changed the character of package tours away from the educational content and towards pure relaxation. This also changed the guides' work specification away from information and towards activities and entertainment. Active learning gave way to more passive forms. The guide became an animator, whose work description included cohesion in the travel group, tension prevention and the provision of good humour (see Cohen, 1985; Falk et al., 2012). Where guides had been involved in *episteme* before, more focus was now put on *techne* and *phronesis*. Tourists learnt how to adapt to new places, increasing their cultural awareness as a form of situated knowledge.

The example of Spies Rejser illustrates Kaiserfeld's argument. The Danish tour operator became very popular in the 1950s when it introduced budget-priced tours to the Mediterranean. The marketing and organization of these tours put the emphasis on relaxation and recreation. The excursions to Spanish destinations included nightlife trips and the famous village fiestas known in Scandinavian languages as "pig parties" since they included a large pork barbecue and as much (cheap) red wine as you pleased (Illum Hansen, 2006). At these sea and sand destinations, guides had a pronounced social function as animators and organizers of various activities. The blockbuster Swedish movie *Sällskapsresan* (*The Package Tour*) depicts iconic 1980s tour guides: guides led workout groups, performed in shows and held parties. They were responsible for fun and enjoyment more than for knowledge provision, as had been the case before. One example is a tourist's review of the "glistening storyteller" Malin on TUI's homepage:

> Malin . . . is a brilliant storyteller. The coach had hardly started rolling when she began entertaining us with stories of past and present Majorca; about pirates, haciendas and vineyards; but also about where Rafael Nadal grew up, and where celebrities like Claudia Schiffer and Michael Douglas have their summer houses.
>
> (TUI, 2021, authors' translation)

The quote shows the varied character of guiding in mass tourism. Tourists are provided with entertaining stories, historical facts, gastronomic heritage and contemporary gossip. Although most tour operators included excursions to places of cultural significance, the mediation of formal knowledge was not at the forefront. However, the "mass tourists" accumulated significant amounts of cultural learning when travelling to the Mediterranean. The tourist experience had, for instance, a large impact on Scandinavian culinary habits. Swedes and Danes started to eat pasta, vegetables and barbecued meat; they even started to enjoy wine. Such habits had previously been rare outside the urban elites. This represents another form of learning, a form of practical knowledge where cultural awareness is based on encounters with people and places. In such cases, guides and guiding only play indirect roles.

Tourism continued to grow and as more and more people travelled, tourism became more diverse. There appeared to be many possibilities for people with all sorts of special interests to delve into the transformative possibilities of learning. Learning was viewed positively, instead of as being something you have to do (see Cavender et al., 2020). The Swedish tour operator Temaresor is an interesting example of this. It was started in 1971 as "Birdwatchers' Travel" by a human geographer from Lund, Sweden (Jeanson, 2019). It now offers a combination of hiking and biking tours, nature tours and cultural travel. Temaresor is clearly targeting customers who demand high quality. On its homepage, guides are shown with names and portraits, education, special qualifications and a short note about themselves (Temaresor, 2021). Academic knowledge and geographic acquaintance are highlighted qualities, promising a high-quality experience that opens up possible learning situations.

Tourism in the digital age

Guiding and learning have been highly influenced by the parallel developments of globalization and digitization. Some guiding has become more diverse and multifaceted, and also more context-specific. On such tours, guides need relevant insights into place-specific contexts (geography, history and service provisions), and specific knowledge about the chosen topic of the tour (Weiler & Black 2015). For example, two researchers in geology and meteorology could be invited as guides on a tour to the glaciers of Svalbard, being able to answer particular questions about the formation of snow and long-term weather developments in the Arctic (author's own knowledge; see also chapter 6 in this book). In tours like this, detailed facts are at the centre of interest, and participants pay a lot in terms of money, preparation time and dedication to take part in such themed guided tours.

Another development path is linked to travel for the upkeep of personal relations. In the stream of globalization, many families are split around the world. Mobility levels are high, and more and more people speak of having more than one home. Such connections are maintained by digitization. Travel to the people you like and love are becoming more common (Gösslin et al., 2018; Zillinger, 2021a). Tourism has become an activity that may not be aimed at a specific topic or place, but that is done in order to visit friends and relatives. Here, learning becomes a by-product, a passive experience where the focus is on doing things together. Taking part in a guided tour is a popular activity. The chosen places may not be of the greatest importance in themselves. The interesting point is that guided tours enable togetherness – just like taking a walk without a guide. The guide acts as the glue that keeps individuals together in order to share their time. By doing so, the guide indirectly contributes to producing memorable experiences. People taking part in such guided tours have a rather serendipitous accumulation of information and knowledge. New knowledge can be acquired, but does not necessarily have to be.

The latest decades cannot be presented without discussing the deep effects that digitization has had – on tourism and on society as a whole. Digitization both influences distinct aspects of tourist behaviour, among them guiding, and it also permeates the tourist system as a whole (Dredge, 2018; Zillinger 2021b). As global digitization and the growth of tourism go hand in hand, Xiang (2018, p. 147) speaks of an "accelerating age of digitalization." The continuing progress of digitization influences not only tourist behaviour but also the supply side of tourism, including guided tours and the information they convey to their participants. One novel type of guiding is the free guided tour, in which fees are replaced by voluntary tips by the participants (del Pilar Leal Londono & Medina, 2017; Nilsson & Zillinger, 2020). Free guided tours were introduced in Berlin in 2003, offering an informal guiding style. The tour companies are often organized in "phygital" ways (Mieli, 2022), involving both physical and digital networks. They are often managed by economies of scope. This means that the structure of a tour and its marketing is copied to other places.

So who are the guides? Data for these paragraphs are partly derived from a study in the cities of Berlin, Copenhagen, Tallinn and Warsaw (Nilsson & Zillinger, 2020), but random sampling from other cities such as Amsterdam, Budapest and London confirm these findings. Guides in free walking tours combine low levels of formal education with high levels of geographical capital. Many consider themselves as cosmopolitans. Authorized guide training is considered unnecessary, as the information circulated during the tours is cordial, pleasant and informal. For example, the Berlin guide Daphna wants to "share my love for the city with travellers who want to find a different side to the city" (Original Europe Tours, 2019). Jakob from Copenhagen "has been travelling and touring in Europe with his rock bands and as a solo artist, and he obviously loves to entertain people" (Copenhagen Free Walking Tours, 2019). Guides who want to establish meaningful relationships with their participants have been labelled relational guides (Bryon, 2012). In Berlin and other places, they are freelancers with great passion for their place of residence. Relational guides usually work on an individual basis, but are included in physical and digital networks, in which the roles of colleagues and friends are blurred. The guiding organization acts as a social arena, and friendly relationships are coveted both with other guides and with tourists.

Free guided tours around the globe are contrasted with traditional tours, based on official fees. The alleged differences build both on content and on participants. Very simply, the aim is to entertain and not to bore: infotainment is the fundamental idea. Free tours also claim to be authentic due to the guides' place attachment, with a mix of official information and personal stories (Widtfeldt Meged & Zillinger 2018). For example, the Berlin guide Jamin aims to "show travellers . . . a fun and social experience of the true alternative scene in Berlin" (Original Europe Tours, 2019). Local knowledge is regarded as better knowledge due to its higher levels of authenticity (Nilsson & Zillinger, 2022). Who is interested in data derived from encyclopaedias? In this sense, the transferred knowledge is tacit rather than implicit, and it changes from day to day, as in this example from Sandemans: "No two tours are alike, and the sites, stories, and length of the tour will vary depending on what your guide decides is best. That's why the tours we promote never get stale or feel scripted, and why savvy travellers prefer SANDEMANs" (Sandemans New Europe, 2019).

The attractions on free guided tours resemble those on other sorts of tours. Most of the places selected have a high level of recognition based on either 20th-century history or popular culture. Tour participants learn about alternative culture and street art, and mundane themes include pub evenings, where guides and participants go out and party (cf. the village fiestas during mass tourism). In cities with a history of war and political turmoil, many stories relate to the inhabitants' daily suffering during those times. The places included on the tours are well known to a greater public, they are emblematic and of high symbolic power. The knowledge included is a relationship between political situations, history and everyday lives. Needless to say, stories build on emotions. One example is the tour to the Palace of Tears in Berlin (Palast der Tränen). Guides tell the story of families who were separated and reunited during the Cold War, a story that consists of grief and contentment. It is about showing the morale of a different era, and is intended to enliven history and place-specific politics. In this way, the tours do consist of theoretical knowledge, but under a surface of emotions and individual human destinies. During such guided tours, tourists are given the opportunity to deepen their knowledge and to make it part of their own lived experience as *phronesis*.

Concluding discussion

This chapter shows that learning plays a central role in tourism, not least in guided tours. Guiding is a vital part of learning when people are travelling as part of guided tours. Learning is an important reason for travel and an essential part of the travel experience. As such, it is often combined with elements of hedonism. The framing of knowledge is in line with present social and cultural developments: enlightenment in the 18th century, industrial exploration of the world in the 19th century and social emancipation in the first half of the 20th century. The post-war period saw a trend away from learning towards hedonistic tourism (Kaiserfeld, 2010). That trend is relative, however, as the number of tourists multiplied in a short period; social and economic emancipation lowered the barriers to participation in tourism, and large numbers of people travelled mostly for leisure. But even package tours that primarily aim for leisure involve elements of learning. This is done in entertaining ways, as in the free guided tours.

This chapter aimed to explore the history of the different roles that guided tours have had, and to explore how such roles have contributed to tourists' learning. In terms of theory, the chapter builds on Cohen's guide categories and on the categories of knowledge which have been related to tourism

(Falk et al., 2012). We do not agree with the chronological development of guides' roles put forward by Cohen (1985). The development is not unidirectional. Instead, all four roles suggested by Cohen are present side by side in most guiding contexts. The roles are complementary, and guides need to perform different roles for a guided tour to be successful. Forms of guiding and of knowledge dissemination depend on both the character and the physical setting of the tour. The destination, where guiding actually *takes place*, is vital for how guiding is performed. Transport is also important for the learning process, as different means of transport have different reach and speed, and allow different kinds of interaction.

Considering Falk et al.'s (2012) conceptualizations of learning, tourists have been presented with all aspects of learning throughout the history of tourism. At first sight, it seems as if theoretical knowledge, *episteme*, is highlighted in guiding: specific information is presented and shared in guiding moments. Practical knowledge, *techne*, comes mainly in the form of passive learning. People develop skills incidentally when practising tourism. They learn to manage security controls at airports, to order food at restaurants, and to navigate through unknown landscapes. They also master new digital tools that enable them to learn more about their destinations. The active learning of practical skills is mainly present during special interest tourism, for instance when a specialist guide teaches people about bird-watching or mountain climbing. The practical knowledge, *phronesis*, acquired during tourism has evidently been an important reason for travelling for a very long time, and is both a result of active and of passive learning.

Analyzing learning situations in different guiding situations, it is reasonable to believe that the various aspects of learning on guided tours build on one another. Learning in the forms of *episteme* and *techne* could be seen as prerequisites for *phronesis* to develop. *Episteme* and *techne* represent knowledge that is transferable between persons, such as from guide to guest. We understand that *phronesis* adds a further step, which results from an inner process where knowledge meets with experience. Therefore, the role of guides differs between diverse sorts of learning. In a way, guides can only deliver information, but genuine knowledge is formed by the individual tourist based on her previous experience and acquaintance. Guides help the tourist to understand the environment: they deliver facts and relate them to history while they are leading the group through a given space. They take care of navigation and integration within the group, they organize services and make selections, all at once. By integrating the different roles that Cohen (1985) has identified, they enable tourists' active and passive learning of information and knowledge on different levels: *episteme*, *techne* and *phronesis*. Although marketing, organization and business models have been digitized in the past few decades,

many parts of the guiding practice have remained the same. Human interaction and learning are still the essence of guiding. Guides have not been
replaced by digital guiding applications, although this is technically possible. Our historical perspective on guiding shows that tourists are fond
of guides who tell personal stories. Tourists want a leader for their group,
although the reason for this is not the obvious dangers anymore. Instead,
guiding builds on a dialogue which may vary from place to place. Local
guides offer an insight into environments that are strange to tourists – and
here we return to the "strange country" mentioned in the introduction to
this chapter. Guides interpret several aspects of these "strange" places.
Hence, they offer both social and physical accessibility to the unknown
backstage of local communities. In this regard, they act as original guides.
The development of guided tours and of guides' roles does not follow one
clear trajectory, as indicated by Cohen. Today's "smart" tourists (but in a
way, who is not a smart tourist?) favour a casual guiding style based on
infotainment. But as we have seen, infotainment has been an important
element in guiding for a long time.

References

Baedeker, K. (1878). *Paris und seine Umgebungen, nebst den Eisenbahn-Routen nach Paris*. Leipzig: Karl Baedeker.

Brodsky-Porges, E. (1981). The grand tour. Travel as an Educational Device 1600–1800. *Annals of Tourism Research*, 8(2), 171–186. https://doi.org/10.1016/0160-7383(81)90081-5

Broomhall, S., Pitman, T., Majocha, E., & McEwan, J. (2010). *Articulating Lifelong Learning in Tourism: Dialogue between Humanities Scholars and Travel Providers*. Strawberry Hills NSW: Australian Learning and Teaching Council.

Bryon, J. (2012). Tour guides as storytellers – From selling to sharing. *Scandinavian Journal of Hospitality and Tourism*, 12(1), 27–43. https://doi.org/10.1080/15022250.2012.656922

Cavender, R., Swanson, J. R., & Wright, K. (2020). Transformative travel: Transformative learning through education abroad in a niche tourism destination. *Journal of Hospitality, Leisure, Sport & Tourism Education*, 27, 100245. https://doi.org/10.1016/j.jhlste.2020.100245

Cederberg, B. (2015). *Turistens blick. Nedslag i resandets historia*. Lund: Lund Historiska Media.

Cohen, E. (1985). The tourist guide. The origins, structure and dynamics of a role. *Annals of Tourism Research*, 12(1), 5–29.

Copenhagen Free Walking Tours (2019). www.copenhagenfreewalkingtours.dk.

Dredge, D. (2018). *Digitalisation in Tourism*. Denmark: Aalborg University.

Falk, J. H., Ballantyne, R., Packer, J., & Benckendorff, P. (2012). Travel and learning: A neglected tourism research area. *Annals of Tourism Research*, 39(2), 908–927. https://doi.org/10.1016/j.annals.2011.11.016.

Gössling, S., Cohen, S. A., & Hibbert, J. F. (2018). Tourism as connectedness. *Current Issues in Tourism*, 21(14), 1586–1600. https://doi.org/10.1080/13683500.20 16.1157142

Gråbacke, C. (2008). *När folket tog semester. Studier av Reso 1937–1977*. Lund: Sekel.

Hannavy, J. (2012). *The Victorian and Edwardian Tourist*. London: Shire Library

Hobsbawm, E. (1981). *Kapitalets tidsålder* [The Age of Capital]. Stockholm: Tiden.

Illum Hansen, A. (2006). *Spies, rejs og vaer glad – livsglaede gennem 50 år*. Copenhagen: Forlaget Saxo.

Jeanson, N. R. (2019). Founder of Temaresor, personal communication.

Kaiserfeld, T. (2010). From sightseeing to sunbathing: Changing traditions in Swedish package tours; from edification by bus to relaxation by airplane in the 1950s and 1960s. *Journal of Tourism History*, 2(3), 149–163. https://doi.org/10.1080/1 755182X.2010.523147

Koshar, R. (1998). What ought to be seen: Tourists' guidebooks and national identities in modern Germany and Europe. *Journal of Contemporary History*, 33(3), 323–340. www.jstor.org/stable/261119

MacCannell, D. (1973). Staged authenticity: Arrangements of social space in tourist settings. *American Journal of Sociology*, 79(3), 589–603. www.jstor.org/stable/2776259

Mieli M. (2022). Phygital. In D. Buhalis (Ed.), *Encyclopedia of Tourism Management and Marketing*. Cheltenham: Edward Elgar Publishing.

Nilsson, J. H. (2012). Hospitality in aviation. A genealogical study. *Hospitality & Society*, 2(1), 77–98. https://doi.org/10.1386/hosp.2.1.77_1

Nilsson, J. H. (2016). *Hotellens och krogarnas framväxt. Ett kulturgeografiskt perspektiv*. Örebro: Örebro Universitet.

Nilsson, J. H., & Zillinger, M. (2020). Free guided tours: Storytelling as a means of glocalizing urban places. *Scandinavian Journal of Hospitality and Tourism*, 20(3), 286–301. https://doi.org/10.1080/15022250.2020.1772866

Nilsson, J. H., & Zillinger, M. (2022). Free guided tours. In D. Buhalis (Ed.), *Encyclopedia of Tourism Management and Marketing*. Cheltenham: Edward Elgar Publishing

Original Europe Tours (2019). www.originalberlintours.com.

Oxford English Dictionary (1933). *Guide*. Vol. IV. Oxford English Dictionary. Clarendon.

Rotberg, R. I. (1970). *Africa and its Explorers: Motives, Methods, and Impact*. Cambridge: Harvard University Press.

Sandemans New Europe (2019). www.neweuropetours.eu/.

Saugstad, T. (2005). Aristotle's contribution to scholastic and non-scholastic learning theories. *Pedagogy, Culture & Society*, 13(3), 347–366. https://doi.org/10.1080/14681360500200233

Swinglehurst, E. (1982). *Cook's Tours. The Story of Popular Travel*. London: Blandford Press.

Temaresor (2021). www.temaresor.se.

TUI (2021). www.tui.se/inspiration/utflykt-drakgrottorna-pa-mallorca

on Seth, T. (2008). *Charterhistoria*. Sweden: Vivlio förlag.

Weiler, B., & Black, R. (2015). *Tour Guiding Research*. Bristol: Channel View Publications.

Widtfeldt Meged, J., & Zillinger, M. (2018). Disruptive network innovation in guided tours. *Scandinavian Journal of Hospitality and Tourism*, 18(3), 303–318. https://doi.org/10.1080/15022250.2018.1497317

Xiang, Z. (2018). From digitalization to the age of acceleration: On information technology and tourism. *Tourism Management Perspectives* 25(1), 147–150. https://doi.org/10.1016/j.tmp.2017.11.023

Zillinger, M. (2021a). Resande – en del av vardagen i ett globalt samhälle. *Organisation och Samhälle*. 2, 28–34.

Zillinger, M. (2021b). *Tourism revisited: The influence of digitalisation on tourism concepts*. Report Series ETOUR Working Paper. Mid Sweden University. www.miun.se/Forskning/forskningscentra/etour/nyheter/nyhetsarkiv/2021-9/malin-zillinger/

Zuelow, E. G. E. (2016). *A History of Modern Tourism*. New York: Palgrave.

5 Experience-based learning through archaeological information panels

Using heritage interpretation

Maria Persson and Anita Synnestvedt

All over the world, information panels are set up in order to inform visitors about archaeological heritage sites. In fact, the information panel is often the only information a heritage visitor receives. Thus, it is central to people's experience of archaeological sites. Even in the digital age, the information panel has unique possibilities for shaping people's experience of heritage sites and contributing to experience-based on-site learning. The information panel can engage the visitor, be a facilitator for knowledge and an eye-opener into time and space. Nevertheless, information panels as interpretive media are rarely problematized within heritage research (see Baram, 2019; Gustafsson & Karlsson, 2004; Högberg, 2013; Synnestvedt, 2013), nor is the question raised as to how they can be developed to contribute to learning for the site-visiting tourist.

In this chapter we put forward the concept of heritage interpretation as a methodological approach that can foster experience-based learning (see chapter 1) and communicate archaeological knowledge (Ham, 2013; Synnestvedt, 2008). Heritage interpretation is about mediating knowledge in a way that engages the audience. The goal is to make heritage meaningful and relevant on a personal and emotional level. This can be done through many different interpretive media in which a heritage consumer takes part in the interpretation. In this chapter we focus on archaeological information panels as communication channels for conveying archaeological knowledge to the tourist. Hence, this chapter has two purposes: to investigate the information panel as a communication channel for archaeological knowledge within the tourism spectrum and to explore how heritage interpretation can foster archaeological experience-based learning – using information panels as an example.

The chapter starts with a short introduction to archaeological tourism activities and their connection to knowledge communication and experience-based learning. Thereafter, the concept of heritage interpretation is introduced. The focus is on the TORE model, developed by Sam

DOI: 10.4324/9781003293316-5

lam (2013), which has four components that form the basic preconditions for successful heritage interpretation. This is followed by a section about archaeological information panels, including their development over time, their present state of the art and their potential for development. In the final part of the chapter, the TORE model is used to discuss how archaeological information panels can be developed in order to engage the audience and contribute to experience-based learning. This is applied to the archaeological site of Tumlehed, a prehistoric rock-painting site in Sweden.

Archaeotourism as a learning activity

Most people experience heritage sites in the role of tourists, or when spending leisure time at heritage sites in their local environment. A large part of heritage tourism is archaeotourism – travel that focuses on visiting and experiencing archaeological sites (Baram, 2008; McGettigan & Rozenkiewicz 2013). Archaeology is even recognized as one of the prime assets within today's tourist industry (Timothy & Tahan, 2020). Several conflicts of interest between the positive and negative effects of archaeotourism have been acknowledged (for recent examples see Comer & Willems, 2019; Timothy & Tahan, 2020). On the one hand, there is a risk of commodification of archaeological heritage and damage to archaeological sites due to increased visitor numbers. On the other hand, there are many benefits. Archaeotourism offers numerous job opportunities all around the world. Also, and highly related to knowledge and learning, tourism is an undercommunicated outreach opportunity for archaeological knowledge and science.

Archaeotourism includes a range of activities, such as visiting museum exhibitions, taking part in live guided tours of monuments and sites, augmented reality experiences or visiting an archaeological site by yourself and taking part in archaeological interpretation through *in situ* information panels. All these activities are based on the communication and consumption of archaeological knowledge, and are recognizable as archaeological learning activities. One thing they all have in common is that they are learning activities that take place outside the normative learning spaces (such as classrooms) and they focus on experience. It should be added that schools also use archaeological sites within their formal learning activities, an aspect not discussed in this chapter.

Experience-based learning covers learning processes through which the participant constructs knowledge, skills and values through direct experiences. Learning that takes place outside normative learning spaces, as for example at a heritage site, is often more effective since we reflect on concrete experiences (Kolb, 1984). Experiential learning is based on the assumption that knowledge is formed and reshaped through experiences.

You construct knowledge through experiences, and you test your knowledge adding new experiences. Applied to a consumer perspective, experiential learning should be produced with the consumer's previous experience and knowledge in mind, since we learn in relation to our previous knowledge and experience. Experiential learning in heritage contexts can create meaning in different ways; it increases awareness of cultural heritage and can contribute to personal development for the individual (Henson, 2017). The latter refers to the social significances of cultural heritage, which includes feelings of context and belonging in time and space (Jones, 2017). The key to such a process is to enable heritage tourism activities to focus on experience and learning.

Heritage interpretation

Archaeological sites and artefacts do not speak for themselves and the common visitor cannot be expected to have more than basic (if any) knowledge in archaeology. Therefore, archaeological sites are interpreted and mediated by those who have such knowledge (Hodges, 2020), like archaeologists or other representatives of cultural heritage management.[1] One interpretative approach is to use the concept of heritage interpretation.[2] This concerns how the ideas of heritage management about heritage sites, artefacts or landscapes are communicated to an audience. The organization NAI (National Association for Interpretation; USA/Canada) has, through inquiries and feedback from hundreds of colleagues, set a definition of heritage interpretation (2022): "Interpretation is a purposeful approach to communication that facilitates meaningful, relevant, and inclusive experiences that deepen understanding, broaden perspectives, and inspire engagement with the world around us."

Heritage interpretation is a process-driven way of working to bring cultural heritage to life for an audience. In short, this should be done in such a way that the site, the object and the environment feel meaningful and the presentation stimulates the visitor to reflect and be surprised, provoked and amused (Brochu & Merriman, 2011; 2012; Ham, 2013; Pastorelli, 2003; Slack, 2021; Ward & Wilkinson, 2006). Heritage interpretation is carried out using different interpretive media to communicate with the audience. Such media may be personal, such as a guide or live re-enactors. It can also be non-personal, such as, for example, information panels, leaflets and booklets. Lately there has been rapid development of digital techniques for non-personal heritage interpretation, for example through mobile applications and QR codes to communicate information about heritage sites. Analogue information panels, however, are still the most established way of presenting and communicating information about an archaeological site to the public (Baram, 2019; Dicks, 2003; Geijerstam, 1998; Gustafsson & Karlsson, 2004; Högberg, 2013; Synnestvedt, 2008).

Heritage interpretation has its roots in the US National Park Service, where interpretation grew as a way of working to conserve natural resources and to foster public awareness. US National Park Service staff member Freeman Tilden is one of the most influential names associated with the field of interpretation, especially through his seminal book *Interpreting Our Heritage* from 1957. In this book, Tilden unveiled six principles for successful interpretation. Tilden's six principles (1977 [1957]) have become well known and are still commonly used in the field of interpretation.

1   Any interpretation that does not somehow relate what is being displayed or described to something within the personality or experience of the visitor will be sterile.
2   Information, as such, is not Interpretation. Interpretation is revelation based upon information. But they are entirely different things. However, all interpretation includes information.
3   Interpretation is an art which combines many arts, whether the materials presented are scientific, historical or architectural. Any art is in some degree teachable.
4   The chief aim of Interpretation is not instruction, but provocation.
5   Interpretation should aim to present a whole rather than a part, and must address itself to the whole man rather than any phase.
6   Interpretation addressed to children (say up to the age of twelve) should not be a dilution of the presentation to adults, but should follow a fundamentally different approach. To be at its best it will require a separate program.

(Tilden, 1977 [1957], p. 9)

Sam Ham, professor of communication psychology, is an authority in the area of interpretation. He compares the field of interpretation with translating a language for someone who does not know the language (Ham, 1992). He has set up a model for what is required in order to achieve successful interpretation: the TORE model, wherein four components form the basic preconditions for a successful interpretation project:

- Interpretation has a *theme* (T)
- Interpretation is *organized* for easy processing (O)
- Interpretation is *relevant* to the audience (R)
- Interpretation is *enjoyable* to process (E)

Each letter corresponds to a component or quality that the communication needs to have if it is to capture the recipient's attention and reach out with its message. According to Ham (1992, 2013) and many others working within the field of interpretation (Brochu & Merriman, 2011, 2012; Pastorelli, 2003; Slack 2021; Ward & Wilkinson, 2006), selecting a theme is central to all interpretation projects and consists of a main message that you want to convey. Based on the theme, relevant facts are selected. The theme must be chosen based on its possibility of leading to reflection for the relevant audience. Further, in the model, interpretation must be organized in a clear way so that the audience can follow it. In the case of a text, this means that it must be understandable and structured. Ham (2013) has compared this to attaching a bit of Velcro to each piece of knowledge you present and then attaching each of the pieces to a larger idea which the audience is already familiar with.

If the interpretation is to be relevant, Ham states, it needs two qualifications: meaningfulness and personality. Things make sense to us if we can relate them to something familiar. If interpretation elaborates upon something we cannot relate to at all, we tend to feel that it is pointless and it will not awaken an interest (Ham, 1992, 2013). Freeman Tilden also mentions this in his first principle, where he develops the idea that there must be a connection between the interpreter and the recipient (Tilden, 1977 [1957]). Therefore, making people reflect on their own lives and their own experiences creates a relationship with the people with whom you are communicating. Finally, interpretation also needs to be enjoyable. This does not mean that interpretation has to be fun, but rather that it should be engaging and enable a strong experience. This can involve being emotionally affected, sad or worried, for example, when visiting a site of difficult heritage such as a war-related site or an endangered natural area.

Information panels: a Swedish perspective

An information panel is the most common communication channel for archaeological knowledge and usually the only channel for knowledge and learning that the heritage tourist takes part in. Hence, it is central to people's experiences of ancient monuments and archaeology. Information panels might seem like an old-fashioned and analogue communication channel in a digital world, like a communication channel from the past. They also risk being a static medium, often in place for 25 or even 50 years, not changing when society and/or sites change and new scientific findings are revealed. Nevertheless, they are still important and of vital interest for heritage research, cultural heritage management and, at their best, also for the tourist. Being a site-based interpretive media, the panel captures the 'isitor's attention at the site, providing information, while ideally the text and images encourage the visitor to observe and ponder about the site. In erms of enabling learning experiences for the tourist, the information panel has the possibility to function as an "in-situ teaching tool" (Baram, 2019). In order to better understand how information panels are, or should be, designed today, we will start by looking back at the development of information panels at archaeological heritage sites over time, from a Swedish perspective.

The development of information panels

Communicating and consuming knowledge about archaeology and heritage sites through information panels has a very long tradition. In Sweden, it is a hundred-year-old practice. Interestingly enough, this development also follows the growth of tourism. The National Heritage Board[3] (NHB) set up the first archaeological information panels as early as the 1920s. These signs were often triangular, not entirely different from the warning signs used in traffic (Geijerstam, 1998). They were also meant to have a warning character, advising visitors that law protects archaeological sites, rather than providing information about the archaeological site itself (see Figure 5.1).

In the 1930s, we see the first connection between information panels and tourism, as the Swedish Tourism Association began to place panels at ancient monuments at that time. In the early 1940s, the NHB placed orientation signs along the roadsides, to guide motorists to ancient monuments. During the 1950s and 1960s, welfare, motoring and the statutory holiday weeks increased, and with them also tourism. This is reflected in the increase in information signs along the roads, and in the ambition, albeit modest, to turn the ancient monuments into knowledge destinations.

Until then, the panels had not really included any information text about the ancient monuments. The panel had simply informed people about the existence of an archaeological monument, without much further information. This changed during the 1960s when the warning signs were replaced or supplemented with chronological and quantitative information texts about the ancient monument. From the 1970s to the 1990s, a large number of archaeological information panels were set up in Sweden. There was a clear movement away from the warning signs. Instead, there was an ambition to convey information and knowledge, although this was relatively standardized and unvarying from one site to the other. Up until the 1980–1990s, the work on archaeological information signs was mostly under the administration of the central authority, NHB. Therefore, a relatively uniform development can be followed throughout the country until the 1980s. From that

Figure 5.1 "Heritage site protected by the law." Information panel without archaeo-
          logical information at archaeological site at Safjället, Sweden.

Photo: Maria Persson

time there was a decentralization process where the administrative responsibility shifted from the central authority of the NHB to county level. Hence,
in the past 20–30 years information panels throughout the country have had
a varying development in layout as well as content (Gustafsson & Karlsson,
2004). What can generally be said, however, is that information panels from
the past 20 years sometimes contain a more reflexive tone that turns to the
visitor and encourages her to think. There is often relatively more text than
on the previous standardized panels. There is also a tendency to tone down
the fact-packed content, although the panels still often contain quantitative
facts and archaeological terminology.

Figure 5.2 The information panel at the Pilane archaeological site, in Sweden, produced in the early 2000s with a postmodern perspective, asking questions of the visitor:

Hidden messages. The names of the people buried here are no longer remembered by anybody – there is nobody to tell the family history – these stories are gone forever. Still, we wonder who these people in the graves might have been. Were they very different from us here today?

Photo: Maria Persson

The archaeological discipline and its interpretations of prehistory change over time. From a disciplinary historical perspective, one can see that information panels in the landscape have been influenced by theoretical trends in archaeology and that these trends can be reflected in the texts. In the period 1970–1990, the texts were commonly short and informative, representing the positivist theories that dominated discussions at universities and in heritage management at that time (Gustafsson & Karlsson, 2004; Hodges, 2020). During the 1980s, there was a paradigm shift in archaeology at the universities, when post-processual trends accelerated, moving away from positivistic structures of thought towards postmodern perspectives. However, it took some time before this found its way into the activities of cultural heritage management in the landscape. At the beginning of the 21st century, the panels tended to be more open to dialogue and allowed the visitors to draw inferences by thinking for themselves, indicating post-processual influences (see Figure 5.2).

Archaeological information panels in today's Swedish cultural landscape

At the time of writing (2021), there are a variety of archaeological informa-tion panels to be found in the Swedish cultural landscape. Different heritage actors are continually setting up new panels. There are also many old infor-mation panels still on duty in the landscape, surprisingly many of them as old as 40–50 years. One previous survey has shown that if there is an infor-mation panel available at a monument or site in the landscape, most visitors will stop and read it, at least for a short while (Andersson & Persson, 2009). An information panel calls for attention and it is understood that the content of the information panel is of vital interest to discuss.

For the Swedish situation, archaeologist Anders Högberg (2013) has car-ried out a larger study where 50 heritage information panels were analyzed. The study considered layout, text and illustrations in order to investigate the panels' narratives and their relationship to assumptions about prior knowledge. The focus of the study was to investigate how heritage information, through the way in which it is presented, can include or exclude the recipient of the information (Högberg, 2013). The study showed that the panels that work well had straightforward and clear language (more difficult terms are explained) and provided detailed information about the archaeological site. The informa-tion was also based on site-specific knowledge, not general knowledge, as for many information panels. The panels that functioned badly provided inade-quate information; the text was unclear or contradictory or even had bad gram-mar. In addition, these panels were poorly adapted to what prior knowledge could be assumed, since many of them could be defined as requiring "Swed-ish cultural capital." The study showed that the information panels were often aimed at a reader with a cultural identity and understanding that coincides with Swedish elementary school. The knowledge content on the panels therefore risks working poorly for Swedes born abroad and for foreign tourists.

At the core of experience-based learning is the assumption that our learn-ing outcome is related to our previous experiences. The information panel must therefore work well both in relation to our previous knowledge and in delivering interesting new knowledge. This is a challenge. The space on the information panel is limited (approximately 20 lines), which makes the demands on form, material and content exceptionally hard. Often there are also texts in additional languages (for Swedish context, often in English and maybe also in German). The texts in the additional languages are often shorter and are aimed at other target groups with different prior knowledge.

Several complex ingredients are needed if a panel is to function as intended – as an educational tool and a guide to knowledge about a heritage site. Besides the text, other factors also affect the visitors' learning possibilities. This might include, for example, the size of the panel, colours, fonts and font size, as well is images and other illustrations such as maps. Many archaeological panels are complemented with some kind of illustration, often paintings showing persons undertaking prehistoric activities, such as funeral ceremonies or work at a settlement site. The illustration should be regarded as part of the knowledge mediation and can be crucial for the visitor who cannot read the text, such as a child, someone with reading difficulties or a visitor who does not know any of the languages on the panel.

The TORE model in practice

At the archaeological site of Tumlehed, on a flat vertical rock sloping slightly inwards, there is a very well-preserved rock painting from the Stone Age (see Figure 5.3). It was first discovered in 1974 and is one of a

Figure 5.3 The rock painting at Tumlehed, Gothenburg, Sweden.
Photo: Maria Persson

few rock paintings in southern Sweden. It has several outstanding motifs. The largest motif depicted is a red deer. There are also five fish or sea mammals, four boats, six zigzag lines, anthropomorphic (humanlike) figures and a net figure. The rock painting covers an area of about two square metres. It was painted using a red-brown pigment. The lines are about two centimetres wide. This width indicates that the painting was probably made using colour-dipped fingers.

The rock painting at Tumlehed has recently been redocumented by archaeologists from the University of Gothenburg, using new documentation techniques such as digital and infrared photography and image enhancement (Schulz Paulsson et al., 2019). This resulted in the discovery of several previously unknown motifs and details. For example, one of the boats has an elk-head stern. The anthropomorphic figures were also discovered at this time. The painting was made in an archipelago landscape of the Stone Age, with the sea just below it. Today, however, the sea is not even visible from the site, due to shoreline displacement. Nevertheless, the painting should be regarded in a maritime perspective. It has been dated to somewhere between 4200 and 2500 BCE. There are several Stone Age settlement sites in the area, the most famous of them just a couple of minutes away from the painting on foot.

As described, there is a long history of human presence at Tumlehed. We will use this site to discuss and exemplify how the TORE model can be used to develop engaging and meaningful knowledge communication through information panels, in a way that facilitates experience-based learning. At present, there is an information panel from the 1970s placed near the painting. It contains some information about the presumed date of the rock painting, comparisons with Bronze Age rock carvings and an illustration in black and white of the motifs on the rock – as known at that time (see Figure 5.4).

Choosing a theme

We begin with choosing a theme, which is the starting point of an interpretation project. A theme is a certain idea that you want to communicate, and is not the same as a topic. A topic is more general and could be, for example, the Stone Age, rock paintings or excavations. A theme is rather the overall conclusion that you want the audience to take away with them after they have taken part in the interpretation. We chose the theme "Humans and their need for artistic expression" for Tumlehed. The ancient paintings at the site are inspiring and the immediate questions are why, how and for whom these paintings were made. Similar questions could be asked regarding present-day graffiti, for example. All humans in all times have had the need to express their lives and traditions in different ways: paintings, dance,

Figure 5.4 The current information panel at Tumlehed.
Photo: Maria Persson

music, stories, objects, clothes, food and so on. A theme like this can be related to human existential questions in many ways, relevant to any human being regardless of age, cultural background or ethnic belonging. When the theme has been decided, facts can be chosen to support the theme and build up the story.

The need for organization

Interpretation should be arranged and presented in a way that is easy for the audience to follow. It needs to be carefully organized. When it comes to exemplify how the TORE model can archaeological information panels, this concerns both the actual text and other aspects of the information panel. For example, the location of the information panel at the archaeological site is crucial. The location determines the reader's place and view while reading. Of course, the information panel should be placed where the visitors can discover it. It must also be placed so that the actual monuments or sites are visible from the location of the panel, although there are many examples of this not being the case. There is also the aspect of accessibility. Working with accessibility plans is a large topic that we do not develop further in this context. However, the information panel should be placed so that as many people as possible can approach it and partake of its educational potential. An information panel is supposed to function in all kinds of weather. It might be in place for many years without any need for change or repair. Unfortunately, the visitor is quite often met with an information panel in bad shape, often impossible to read, or even with only the pole and frame intact. This is clearly bad organization.

At Tumlehed there is a need for good organization since the paintings are not very easily accessible; you need to climb up a steep mountain on a small, narrow and slippery path. It is not possible for everybody to reach the painting and see the current information panel. The organization at this site should consider an information panel below the rock with the painting visually accessible for those who cannot climb up the steep hill. There should also be another panel at the top, close to the painting, with somewhat different messages from those on the panel below and with updated information related to the latest scientific research (see Schulz Paulsson et al., 2019).

When it comes to the text on the panels, it is important for it to be easy to understand for the audience, not hard to follow, too dense or too complicated. In connection to the TORE model, Ham states that most people can take in up to a maximum of four different pieces of information at the same time (Ham, 2013). If your interpretation is not limited to that, you risk losing your audience due to too much information. At the Tumlehed site we would choose as our four pieces or lines of information the motifs, the maritime context, new research through new techniques and how the paintings were probably made. We would also illustrate this in a picture on the information panels, depicting a person creating the painting, the new documentation visualizing all the figures on the rock, and with the sea depicted just below the site.

How to make the interpretation relevant

Interpretation needs to be relevant for the audience. Information that we regard as relevant should have two characteristics: it should be *meaningful* and it should be *personal* (Ham, 2013). If information is to be perceived as meaningful, it should relate to previous experience and knowledge. This means that you have to know your audience to be able to make successful heritage interpretation. This leads us to consider to whom the archaeological knowledge and information panels are directed. In Sweden the receiver can be expected to be Swedish or foreign tourist, the latter probably of north European origin (Andersson & Persson, 2009; Högberg, 2013). However, the concept of archaeological heritage sites includes everything from UNESCO World Heritage Sites, with a high number of foreign tourists, to a local site not known to a larger audience outside the local community. Once again, communication should be adapted to the presumed recipient in order to be relevant.

Information can also lack meaning if too many technical terms or abbreviations are used (Ham, 2013). It has been common for Swedish archaeological information panels to contain a text according to a standard form in three points, mainly focusing on precisely these points: chronology, archaeological terminology and technical information (Geijerstam, 1998). This standard has to some extent been abandoned in modern information panels. Today, more emphasis is placed on describing the context and activities that might have taken place at the archaeological site (Geijerstam, 1998).

Interpretation is also relevant to the audience when it is personal. This is acknowledged in Tilden's first principle, namely that interpretation that does not relate to something within the personality or experience of the visitor will be sterile (Tilden, 1977 [1957]). Interpretation needs to connect to something that the audience cares about. This might sound very difficult to accomplish, especially when the audience is not known, as at an unstaffed heritage interpretation site with an information panel. One way to accomplish this is to focus on timeless, universal questions and feelings which most people can connect to (Ham, 2013). Archaeologist Cornelius Holtorf has suggested that archaeologists contribute most to the experience of society when they tell stories (Holtorf, 2010). This may be stories about how things were in the past or about archaeological practice. However, more important, Holtorf argues, are the meta-stories of archaeology. Such stories originate in archaeology and the past but focus on the people of today. He suggest three themes for meta-stories: what it means to be human, who we are as members of a particular human group and how we might be living under different circumstances (Holtorf, 2010). These are timeless questions applicable to both past and present societies, giving meaning and personal experiences to people of today through the use of archaeology. This is highly applicable to heritage interpretation through archaeological information panels and Tumlehed is no exception. Timeless questions could easily be presented at the suggested panels at the site; didactic questions might be used, such as by whom, why, when and for whom the paintings were made and how artistic expressions such as the rock painting make it possible for us today to connect to humans of the past.

It has to be enjoyable

Last in the TORE model is the quality that interpretation needs to be enjoyable to process. This means that it should be engaging and enable strong experiences. It often involves being emotionally affected. Using a theme like *Humans and their need for artistic expression* can also be linked to Tilden's fourth principle: the chief aim of interpretation is not instruction, but provocation. If, for example, you were to compare graffiti with the ancient paintings, this would probably provoke many people, but it would also get people involved, affected, and inspire new insights and reflections. That is why we have chosen this theme for Tumlehed. It is a universal theme that everybody can relate to in one way or another.

Another relatable perspective at Tumlehed is the changes in the landscape, which is a very urgent and engaging topic for discussion. At this site it is possible to imagine the Stone Age sea level, much higher than today. This can easily be connected to present concerns about sea level rise due to climate change. Trying to understand previous landscapes and how they were used by people of the past gives new perspectives on this. These perspectives can also be connected to our chosen theme for the site. Human artistic expressions might last or disappear. This very old artistic expression has coincidentally been conserved through the millennia, enabling us to partake of this prehistoric artistic expression. Do we make art for the moment or for eternity? Do we make it for ourselves or for others? At its best, heritage interpretation makes people reflect on their own lives.

Meaning-making learning experiences for the tourist: using heritage interpretation

Our aim in introducing you to the Tumlehed archaeological site was to highlight the TORE model and to give insights on how to use and think about the model. Our choice of theme is entirely ours, and could have been a very different one if chosen by others.

Experiences are based, for example, on stories, interaction and presence, and experiences that create personal meaning are more likely to contribute to learning (Falk et al., 2012; Jernsand & Goolaup, 2020). The information panel, though a traditional form of heritage communication, has the potential to shape the perception of a place for tourists and to function as an *in situ* learning tool (Baram, 2019). Since the archaeological site by definition is outdoors in the cultural landscape, this provides good prerequisites or experience-based learning. This takes place outside normative learning spaces and the participant learns through direct experiences and interaction.

Heritage interpretation has many similarities with the concept of experience-based learning as the participant constructs knowledge, skills and values through direct experiences. We suggest that the areas of experience-based learning and heritage interpretation could be a fruitful companionship, enriching each other in developing interesting, enjoyable, engaging and provoking learning activities for tourists. Such a companionship offers both theory (experience-based learning) and methods (heritage interpretation). When it comes to developing information panels in line with this argument, we recognize two main areas of action as starting points.

First, as in all communication, it is crucial to start with your audience and to adapt the message accordingly. The most important concern when using heritage interpretation is that it should relate to experiences and knowledge that are familiar to the specific audience. Hence, we argue that learning more about the visitor at archaeological heritage sites is of the highest priority, in order to develop suitable information panels. Who are the visitors and what prior knowledge can they be expected to have? Every quality in the TORE model is dependent on this knowledge. In concrete terms, more research needs to be done to investigate who the archaeotourist is. This differs from site to site, and interpretation should thus vary more than it does today.

Our second argument is that it is necessary to regard the information panel as more than just that. Information, as such, is not interpretation. Interpretation should be based upon information, but they are different things (Tilden, 1977 [1957]). Cultural heritage management must to abandon its mission to *inform* the visitor. The basic idea of most of the current archaeological knowledge communication on information panels is *to inform by presenting archaeological facts*. To accomplish experience-based learning with information panels as interpretive media, we suggest that the information panel should be regarded more as a door opener to ways of experiencing archaeological heritage, rather than as solely mediating facts about the past. It should be noted, of course, that heritage interpretation should be based on knowledge. It is how this knowledge is communicated that matters.

Although the information panel is an analogue communication channel in a digital age, it still has its incomparable qualities. The information panel is something that greets the visitor to an archaeological site and points out that he or she has reached a site of interest. However, even the analogue information panel has its digital development potentials. New information panels sometimes include information about digital channels where more information and knowledge can be reached. For the time being this is primarily represented by QR codes, directing the visitor to further communication channels such as movies, information texts or museum websites. This enables the analogue sign to lead the audience to the most up-to-date information. It also enables the visitor who wants more in-depth knowledge about the context and the archaeology to reach such information. However, it is the information panel that creates interest in partaking of that enhanced knowledge. Directing the site-visiting tourist from the analogue information panel to digital communication channels is an area with interesting possibilities. This can make the information panel less static and open to further experience-based learning.

The information panel can be a facilitator for knowledge and a door-opener into the time and space of the archaeological site. It is also the most common way to communicate archaeological knowledge to tourists visiting archaeological sites. However, panels often contain information directed to an unidentified target group and fail to be engaging. Using inspiration from heritage interpretation can contribute to the development of engaging and meaningful knowledge communication and contribute to experience-based learning for the archaeotourist. At the core of heritage interpretation is the ambition to provoke your audience to think for themselves, and thereby to develop an understanding of the subject matter, for example, an archaeological site. The tourist should gain new impressions, thoughts and experiences. Interpretation is about helping people to see, which in turn allows them to learn, explore, make sense of and appreciate archaeological sites. The outcome of such learning experiences will be increased awareness of archaeological heritage and personal development for the tourist.

Notes

1   Cultural heritage management includes decision-making and the administration of cultural heritage. It can be carried out by both private and public actors. The first refers to NGOs, volunteers, local communities and organizations, often referred to as non-authorized heritage management, while the latter refers to councils, museums and other governmental organizations – authorized heritage management.
2   Heritage interpretation is an established profession in, for example, Scotland, the USA, Australia and England, where university and continuing education courses are offered by well-known associations such as Interpret Europe, Interpretation Australia, NAI (National Association for Interpretation [USA/Canada]) and AHI (Association for Heritage Interpretation [Scotland]).
3   Sweden's central administrative agency in the area of cultural heritage.

References

Andersson, L., & Persson, M. (2009). Att följa stigen – en publikundersökning på Blomsholm. In *Situ Archaeologica*, 7, 11–22.
Baram, U. (2008). Tourism and archaeology. In D. M. Pearsall (Ed.), *Encyclopedia of Archaeology* (vol. 3, pp. 2131–2134). Amsterdam/London: Elsevier/Academic Press.

Baram, U. (2019). In an age of heritage signs, encouraging archaeological sites to be cosmopolitan canopies. *Present Pasts*, 9(1), 1–8. https://doi.org/10.5334/pp.79

Brochu, L., & Merriman, T. (2011). *Put the Heart Back in Your Community. Unifying Diverse Interests Around a Central Theme*. Fort Collins, CO: Heartfelt Publications.

Brochu, L., & Merriman, T. (2012). *Personal Interpretation – Connecting Your Audience to Heritage Resources* (3rd ed.). Fort Collins, CO: Heartfelt Publications.

Comer, D. C., & Willems, A. (Eds.). (2019). *Feasible Management of Archaeological Heritage Sites Open to Tourism*. Cham: Springer International Publishing.

Dicks, B. (2003).*Culture on Display. The Production of Contemporary Visibility*. Glasgow: Open University Press.

Falk, J. H., Ballantyne, R., Packer, J., & Benckendorff, P. (2012). Travel and learning: A neglected tourism research area. *Annals of Tourism Research*, 39(2), 908–927. https://doi-org.ezproxy.ub.gu.se/10.1016/j.annals.2011.11.016

Geijerstam, J. (1998). *Miljön som minne: att göra historien levande i kulturlandskapet*. Stockholm: Riksantikvarieämbetet.

Gustafsson, A., & Karlsson, H. (2004). *Plats på scen: kring beskrivning och förmedling av Bohusläns fasta fornlämningar genom tiderna*. Uddevalla: Bohusläns Museum.

Ham, S. H. (1992). *Environmental Interpretation. A Practical Guide for People with Big Ideas and Small Budgets*. Golden, Colorado: North American Press.

Ham, S. H. (2013). *Interpretation. Making a Difference on Purpose*. Golden, CO: Fulcrum Books.

Henson, D. (2017). Archaeology and education. In G. Moshenska (Ed.), *Key Concepts in Public Archaeology* (pp. 43–59). London: UCL Press.

Hodges, S. (2020). Interpreting the past: Telling the archaeological story to visitors. In D. J. Timothy & L. G. Tahan (Eds.), *Archaeology and Tourism: Touring the Past* (pp. 167–185). Blue Ridge Summit/Bristol: Channel View Publications.

Högberg, A. (2013). The voice of the authorized heritage discourse: A critical analysis of signs at ancient monuments i Skåne, southern Sweden. *Current Swedish Archaeology*, 2012(20), 131–167.

Holtorf, C. (2010). Meta-stories of archaeology. *World Archaeology*, 42(3), 381–393.

Jernsand, E. M., & Goolaup. S. (2020). Learning through extra-ordinary experiences. In S. Dixit (Eds.), *The Routledge Handbook of Tourism Experience Management and Marketing* (pp. 173–182). New York: Routledge.

Jones, S. (2017). Wrestling with the social value of heritage: Problems, dilemmas and opportunities. *Journal of Community Archaeology & Heritage*, 4(1), 21–37. https://doi.org/10.1080/20518196.2016.1193996

Kolb, D. (1984). *Experiential Learning: Experience as the Source of Learning and Development*. Englewood Cliffs, NJ: Prentice Hall.

McGettigan, F., & Rozenkiewicz, A. (2013). Case study 2: Archaeotourism – The past is our future? In R. Raj, K. Griffin, & N. Morpeth (Eds.), *Cultural Tourism* (pp. 118–128). Wallingford: CABI. http://doi.org/10.1079/9781845939236.0000

National Association for Interpretation (NAI). (2022). www.interpnet.com/.

Pastorelli, J. (2003). *Enriching the Experience: An Interpretive Approach to Tour Guiding*. Frenchs Forest: Hospitality Press.

Schulz Paulsson, B., Isendahl, C., & Frykman Markurth, F. (2019). Elk heads at sea: Maritime hunters and long-distance boat journeys in late Stone Age Fennoscandia. *Oxford Journal of Archaeology*, 38(4), 398–419. https://doi-org.ezproxy. ub.gu.se/10.1111/ojoa.12180

Slack, S. (2021). *Interpreting Heritage. A Guide to Planning and Practise*. Oxford & New York: Routledge.

Synnestvedt, A. (2008). *Fornlämningsplatsen: kärleksaffär eller trist historia*. Göteborg: Göteborgs universitet.

Synnestvedt, A. (2013). Minnesplatser över glömda kulturer eller platser för aktiviteter. En diskussion om hur vi tolkar och levandegör kulturmiljön. In G. Swensen (Ed.), *Å lage kulturminner: hvordan kulturarv forstås, formes og forvaltes* (pp. 205–226). Oslo: Novus.

Tilden, F. (1977/1957). *Interpreting our heritage* (3rd ed.). Chapel Hill, NC: University of North Carolina Press.

Timothy, D. J., & Tahan, L. G. (Eds.) (2020). *Archaeology and Tourism: Touring the Past*. Blue Ridge Summit & Bristol: Channel View Publications.

Ward, C., & Wilkinson, A. (2006). *Conducting Meaningful Interpretation – A Field Guide for Success* (Fulcrum Applied Communication Series). Golden, CO: Fulcrum Books.

6 Extended ways of experiencing climate change

From photography to virtual reality in Svalbard

Tyrone Martinsson

The past 130 years have seen tourist travels develop in the far north. The basic concept for visiting the islands of Svalbard, in the high Arctic, 800 kilometres north of Tromsø, Norway, remains similar, though. The expected tourist experience includes historical sites, spectacular landscapes with glaciers and ice and encounters with animals, especially the polar bear. Travels in Arctic regions are expensive and are often framed by luxury and a sense of being unique. The crews on ship-based tourist excursions (the most common form of tourism in Svalbard) work hard to give the paying customers an unforgettable experience. This often includes preparing documentations of the trip to be offered to passengers on returning to harbour in the main village of Longyearbyen. Photography is still the most common way of documenting the trips, even though the contemporary capacities of the medium today offer both moving and still images, easily captured by the same camera. Technological developments are rapidly changing and expanding visual options. The use of drones and action cameras is increasing, along with easier photo editing and post-production processes that can be done at home. The technological advances of today link our times with the second half of the 19th century, closing a circle of extending photography and visual observations, moving forward towards future visualizations and virtual technologies that aid our travel to and experiences of remote places. The recent developments in visual technologies open a new era of virtual travel and simulated nature experiences. In this chapter I address the development of visual technologies as tools to aid travel experiences in remote places and give a reflective perspective on that development and its future possibilities from a visual practice perspective.

The tourist experience in the Arctic offers a unique learning opportunity where the impact of climate change is explicitly evident; through direct interaction with the northern environment, visitors are given an on-site explanation of the process of an environment in transition. The Arctic

DOI: 10.4324/9781003293316-6

environment is very sensitive and is severely affected by rising temperatures due to climate change. Both of these parameters affect tourists visiting Arctic destinations. It is impossible today to avoid taking climate change issues and causes into consideration when organizing travels or activities in the Arctic. All serious Arctic tourist operators need to address these issues now, changing the basic outlines for visiting the far north, particularly for safety and environmental protection reasons. I will briefly outline here a framework of visual technology and the experiences offered by its developments. Photography initiated the advanced visual technologies that we have today, offering a fast development of high resolution and quality virtual experiences of remote environments such as the Arctic: a "virtual tourism," as well as a way to visually experience places very difficult to visit. These tools are not only an entertaining experience but they also function as a way of preparing, learning about and understanding the Arctic. This text adds to the contributions of the other chapters in this book on concepts of *experience-based learning* and *transformative learning* as ways of understanding the process involved in tourists' relationship to knowledge and learning, from real life or virtual experiences or a combination of the two.

Methodology

The Arctic is a very different place from anything in southern latitudes. Having joined several tourist ships in Svalbard in different settings between 2011 and 2016, I will reflect on my field experience of those travels. This type of Arctic travel is where this text derives its primary experiences of European Svalbard tourists. As I joined several such trips as a guide in different settings, I will reflect on their arrangements. In addition, I have done extensive fieldwork in Svalbard, where we often encounter tourists visiting the areas where we are working. Such observations from the field are also a basis for this text. Among many methodological approaches within our transdisciplinary framework, two might be highlighted here for the context of this chapter: *Aesthetic Contemplation* (Gernsheim, 1988) and *The Long Story* (Banerjee, 2017; Martinsson, 2021). The first is associated with the study and analysis of photographs, although it is also connected to more philosophical studies of aesthetics which we do not refer to. Contemplation is a way of describing the often complicated play between analyzing archival sources and identifying their contents in the field to create a historical timeline and its connections to visual representations across time. The second approach is inspired by my colleague Professor Subhankar Banerjee at the University of New Mexico. Banerjee developed his concept of the long story in relation to environmental issues and politics. In our latest project, *Extended Rephotography: Immersive Representations of Climate Change,*

we take his concept and develop it in relation to the story of change in landscapes as a long process, occurring over time, influenced by many different
parameters: a story of the natural landscape in relation to human progress
and interactions with that landscape (University of Gothenburg, n.d.). This
text is based on a long set of field observations, writings and visual practice
gathered between 2011 and 2021.

Historical perspectives

In 1819, Lieutenant William Beechey's drawings from Captain David
Buchan's 1818 polar expedition to the North Pole were made into a painted
"virtual tour" in Henry Aston Barker's large rotunda in Leicester Square,
London (see Figure 6.1). The panorama view offered the public the opportunity to experience the north coast of Svalbard (Barker, 1819; Potter, 2007).
The format of a visual display in this large setting was popular; one of
photography's most important inventors, Louis Daguerre, worked on similar technologies based on painting for visual displays and ways of telling.
Twenty years after Beechey's panoramic display, photography was invented

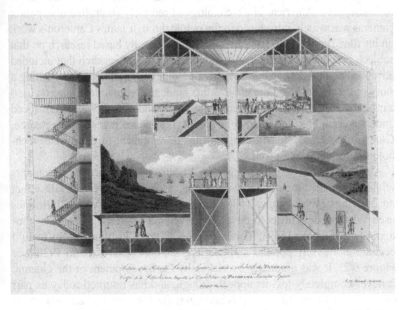

Figure 6.1 Robert Mitchell, architect. Plans and views in perspective. London,
1801. The building of Barker's Panorama.

Source: British Museum

and it did not take long for the new visual technology to be included on major expeditions.

When Sir John Franklin left England in 1845 and vanished in the Canadian Arctic searching for the Northwest Passage, he carried Daguerre's new visual technology on board his ship. Several times during search expeditions and throughout the more than 150 years that passed before the finding of Franklin's two ships, HMS *Terror* in 2014 and HMS *Erebus* in 2016, Inuit had given clues and accounts of locations and traces that were eventually crucial in solving the mystery of that expedition (Barr, 2019). Parks Canada and the Inuit community in Nunavut now work in collaboration with marine archaeological and historical fieldworkers on the locations of the ships. Anyone interested in the complex relationship between native oral traditions, traditional knowledge and Western societies' histories in the Arctic will find great interest in following the findings of Franklin's expedition. The hope of finding photographic material still remains at the time of writing. The whole framing of work in these extreme Arctic waters also carries a narrative relevant to the subject of this chapter, through its use of remote cameras allowing us not only to follow the works of marine archaeologists in the field but to be taken on a unique journey to learn about a historical site at the bottom of the sea and its connection with the clashes of Western colonial ambitions in the Inuit lands of Arctic North America. The technology of remotely controlled underwater cameras was widely introduced to the public through James Cameron's work on his film *Titanic* (1997) and his subsequent visually based research on that subject, introducing marine archaeology and historical research that included advanced equipment capable not only of aiding research but also of telling a story of the findings and the process that made them possible. Cameron used a mixture of 3D animation, stereo-photography and film, as well as advanced underwater filming, and in 2003 he produced a documentary on the research, *Ghost of the Abyss*; he still continues his development of underwater technologies for marine research.

As early as the 1830s, Sir Charles Wheatstone had started experiments with equipment he called a stereoscope, a device to create a 3D effect on drawings (Wheatstone, 1838). In the 1850s, Oliver Wendell Holmes used Wheatstone's ideas to develop his version of stereo viewers in photography (Holmes, 1859). This stereo technology in photography would become immensely popular and had its peak between 1870 and 1920 (see Figure 6.2). It was gradually overtaken by the development of the cinema. It never completely lost its appeal, though, and has returned today as part of the development of digital technologies for both science and entertainment. At the time of writing, Canon has released its new Dual Fisheye Lens, which has the capacity of capturing high-quality views in 180-degree stereo. Mounted on a mirrorless digital camera body, it offers the latest in state

Figure 6.2 The stereograph as educator: Underwood patent extension cabinet in a
home library. Underwood & Underwood, ca. 1901.

Source: Library of Congress

of the arts stereo imaging technology. The capacity of such equipment, producing high-resolution images edited for virtual experiences, both for home
viewing and institutions, extends technologies for bringing the world back
home. Armchair travel is given a new meaning. In field-based research we
see this as an opportunity not only for expanding research options but for
the communication of research findings related to remote areas of the world.

Svalbard: discovery and (tourism) development

In 1596, while searching for eastern trade routes, a Dutch expedition discovered Svalbard. The Dutch originally gave it the name Spitsbergen,
from its shorelines with sharply pointed hills (Beke, 1853, Conway, 1906,
Wieder, 1919) (from the Dutch *spits*, meaning pointed, and *bergen*, meaning mountains). After 1925 Spitsbergen was renamed Svalbard by Norway,
when it gained sovereignty over the islands. Svalbard was not inhabited
prior to its discovery; it has never had an Indigenous population. Due to
the Gulf Stream, northwest Svalbard is unique in its accessible coastlines
being significantly milder than most other places at these latitudes. This
made the area accessible for European exploitation. For almost 300 years
it was primarily explorers and whalers who visited the archipelago. At the
end of the 19th century, tourists began to arrive. In the period from 1890
to 1914, ship-based tourism to Scandinavian Arctic destinations began to
develop. In Germany, *Nordlandfahrt*, or "travels to the north," became
an established concept and Scandinavia, and its northern tip, North Cape,

and further north, Svalbard, became popular destinations. As an example, in 1913 Carl Lausberg published *Das Nordland*, chronicling three cruises towards Scandinavia, and particularly Norway and Svalbard. Lausberg's journey to Svalbard followed an operational agenda of cruises still in place: they visited historic northwest Spitsbergen with Magdalenefjorden, and the remains of the whaling settlement at Amsterdamøya with the Dutch memorial monument raised there in 1906; they then went on to Virgohamna to see the remains of the Swedish Andrée expedition and the American Wellman expedition (Lausberg, 1913). Concepts and ideas of the north have shifted and developed (Wråkberg, 1999; Davidson, 2005). Svalbard was once considered a land of eternal ice, surrounded by cold sea, open for exploitation. The bowhead whale was hunted to extinction, walruses were slaughtered along its coastlines and polar bears were killed in high numbers. A coal mining industry developed that is now finally being closed. Svalbard is a good example of the shifting north, where Western cultures are finally being forced to understand the value of the far north with its unique and fragile ecosystems. The Inuit and northern First Nations have long had this understanding and traditional ecological knowledge as an integral and natural part of their cultures; today they offer us a valuable possibility of learning about sustainable ways of living in the north (Cruikshank, 2005; Dowie, 2017), a part of the world with an intrinsic value and importance for the health of the planet. Eventually, in recent decades more lands have become protected, and Arctic tourism is increasingly framed in environmentally sound arrangements.

Up until the 1950s, tourists encountered a Svalbard consistent with hundreds of years of visual representations and travel writings. Historical sites could be revisited and the land had not changed in any significant way. In the past 30 years this has changed dramatically, with a rapidly warming Arctic. Today, historical visual representations of Arctic destinations such as Svalbard play a very different role than originally intended, as valuable sources for time information on vanishing ice. Since 2010 we have established a collaborative transdisciplinary research platform monitoring the changing landscape in Svalbard's Northwest Spitsbergen National Park, with a focus area spanning from Magdalenefjorden in the south to Fuglefjorden in the north. Supporting this is a vast and diverse archive of images from 19th-century science and travels. Images connected to European tourist cruises to Svalbard provide parts of a visual legacy of ice and the status of glaciers, but also an indication of what viewpoints were prioritized by the cruise ships. The frames of these viewpoints are good indicators of the aesthetic and cultural imaginaries carried by visitors of that time. The beginning of tourist cruises in the 1890s set the agenda for how to operate them and where; ships were used as a comfortable base, onboard photographers joined the crew and landings offered close encounters with glaciers or visits to historical remains of industry and exploration. In the beginning the ships were small, but they grew in size as the years went by and cruise-based tourism developed. The model for contemporary logistics in Arctic "mass tourism" has not changed in any dramatic way since the 1920s; large passenger cruisers are still used, as are protected, organized landings at key sites. The new development has been the concept of a more adventure-oriented tourism and its framing as ecologically aware tourism with an often knowledgeable and active smaller group of visitors wanting an embodied experience of the land, as well as an intellectual framing through guides and accompanying scientists or specialists from various relevant fields. This tourism is characterized by smaller ships but also an exclusivity generated by the high cost of operating such tours in these remote and wild areas. The number of passengers ranges from about 50 to 100, with the more exclusive cruises having about 10 to 20. The latter, fairly expensive travels normally operate on an open bridge policy, where passengers are able to move around the ship and can always enter the bridge and chat with the staff, including the captain. In travel packages aimed at these smaller groups, the awareness of the historical landscape is often based on images and maps from earlier visitors. Photographers often accompany both of these types of travel packages, continuing the tradition from the 1890s. The photographs produced from 1890 and onwards are often used in present-day tours when scientists or guides give lectures at landings, offering a unique on-site experience of shifting views of the land and glaciers in particular. This offers a very direct and clear comparison of changes over time, where we have to relate to the fact that, in both a practical and philosophical sense, we are visiting a different Arctic than our predecessors. Today, travelling to the Arctic regions is visiting ground zero of climate change.

Magdalenefjorden and northwest Spitsbergen

Magdalenefjorden, between Kongsfjorden and Virgohamna, was and is a particularly popular stop, with the Gullybreen Glacier, the spectacular and gravity-defying Hanging Glacier and the bottom glacier, Waggonwaybreen, all within view of the landing site on Gravneset, an old English whaling site with a burial ground (see Figure 6.3). The beach at Gravneset is one of the easiest landing sites in northern Svalbard. From the beach an accessible hike to a close encounter with the ice walls of Gullybreen used to be a common tourist attraction. Today, though, the experience is very different, as the ice walls of Gullybreen no longer exist. Nor does the spectacular scenery of the Hanging Glacier, which in the past offered tourists a more adventurous scramble up the hills towards where it dropped out over the steep mountainside. Gravneset is located in the cove of Trinity Harbour, named

Figure 6.3 Magdalenefjorden, Svalbard, 2011. Tourist ship visiting Gravneset. The smaller vessel is the authors' expedition ship, the MS *Stockholm*.

Photo: Tyrone Martinsson

in 1614 by English hunters led by Robert Fotherby, who claimed the area for King James I (Purchas, 1625). The burial ground on top of the slopes on the northern tip of the peninsula is the source of the name Gravneset (Broke, 1807; NPI, 2003). A large boulder on the beach is a popular marker to include when composing photographic views. Professor Marit Anne Hauan told me in conversations about the 1939 hunters Sally and Waldemar Kræmer, who set up a tent on this site where they sold furs to tourists. In Magdalenefjorden, as well as in other locations, Norwegian trappers set up camps and sold furs and bones as souvenirs (M. A. Hauan, personal communication, April 2021). At historic landing sites, tourists often collected artifacts and bones (even human remains from open graves), and in Virgo-hamna pieces of wood from the remains of the Andrée expedition balloon hangar were popular as memorabilia (Martinsson, 2015). This practice is of course strictly forbidden; if anyone is caught looting grave sites or historical remains, considerable fines are to be expected and possibly a ban from any return to Svalbard. On the grave peninsula, contemporary park rangers have built a hut and monitor tourist traffic in the area in the summertime.

Today, the trail marking the route of decades of tourists walking towards Gullybreen is clearly visible and easy to follow. The Hanging Glacier is gone. Viewing a photograph, dated to about 1926–1931, of tourists walking on the slopes facing Gullybreen, one of the most visited glaciers at that time, we get a sense of what the tourists were offered. The glacier was probably popular due to its massive appearance in the fjord and its land-based views, all easily accessible from the soft, dry landings on Gravneset. The daredevils in the groups of visitors could literally walk up and touch the ice and even take the risk of walking on top of the glacier. Looking back in history, the glacier in the 1920s had the same impressive appearance from the sea, between the mountains, as when the first photograph was taken there by Herbert C. Chermside in 1873. In 1839, when Gaimard's French La Recherche expedition came to the fjord and onboard artist Bartolomey Lauvergne made a panoramic drawing depicting the glacier, it dominated the south coast behind the landing beach. It was part of the ice walls of the land, as described by David Buchan's expedition when they reached the fjord in 1818 (Martinsson, 2019; Martinsson, 2021). The postcard image by Carl Müller & Son of tourists dwarfed by ice on the mountain slopes is a key panel when putting together the visual timeline of the retreat of Gullybreen. The image was published in the May issue of *La Montagne: revue mensuelle du Club alpin francais*, 1932, available in the Gallica database at the National Library of France. It was published as part of an article, "Une Croisiere au Spitzberg," by Suzanne Zaborowska, who chronicled a cruise to Spitsbergen in 1931 on the Hamburg Süd Amerikanische cruiser *Monte Rosa*. There is a possibility that the image, dated between 1926 and 1931, was taken during that cruise. It is an image we have used with contemporary tourist groups in a clear and pedagogical way, showing an example of the massive changes of glacial appearance in northwest Spitsbergen. It is also an important panel in the current creation of a story of Magdalenefjorden and its glaciers as part of creating virtual tours and stereo films of the fjord.

More than ten years ago, Professor Pete Capelotti at Penn State University asked a question about the future of tourist cruisers in Svalbard: how much will the rapidly approaching disappearance of "the eternal ice" affect the next century and a half of Svalbard tourism (Capelotti, 2011)? Capelotti's question is even more relevant today. Destinations such as Magdalenefjorden, highly appreciated with its features of large glaciers surrounded by wild mountains, still offer an extraordinary experience for any visitor. Capelotti's observation of the reality of "the land of eternal ice" rapidly vanishing is of concern to future tourism in Svalbard. In the late 19th century and the first half of the 20th century, visitors' expectations were fully met, with impressive glaciers framing the landscape in the fjords, coherent with the idea of a land of eternal ice and cold, a frozen north.

Visitors were granted an experience of light and colour with the occasional sound of passing birds or calving glaciers breaking the silence of the Arctic. The tourists encountered views often entangled in the poetics of an "Arctic Sublime," a concept developed in Chauncey C. Loomis's now classic polar text. Loomis's concept rests on poetic imaginaries of the Arctic driven by dramatic tales of Western exploration, where immense beauty was paralleled by nature's indifference to human ambition in its power and force, with the darkness and cold in the vast and empty spaces of the hardest lands on Earth. However, Loomis argues that the sublime qualities of the Arctic faded away with modern exploration, mapping and reaching the farthest corners of the frozen north. As science progressed, the north lost its magic appeal (Loomis, 1977). It can be argued, though, that the lure of the north is still there, but in a very different way. The documentary productions and even, to some degree, scientific works carry Loomis's sublime aesthetic quality in their narratives, where the effects of climate change provide a different Arctic imaginary, one where humans, with our impact on the planet and anthropocentric relationship with the natural world, are now the threatening force in the Arctic beauty and wildness, reminding us of the vulnerability of nature.

Extended ways of telling

The development of new technologies and environmental challenges for the tourist operators in Svalbard is likely to affect not only the ways of telling about the north but also the practice of field tours with active landings and on-site experiences. In September 2021 the Norwegian Environmental Agency published "Proposed changes to the regulations in Svalbard" Environmental Agency (2021), because climate change and increased tourism are challenging the current environmental policy of the archipelago. The number of tourists disembarking in Svalbard increased from 29,600 in 1996 to 124,000 in 2019. Based on this fact, Norwegian authorities need to act to maintain the protection of Svalbard; the jury for the changes is out in this case and expected outcomes are scheduled in spring 2022.

From our research platform we can see a possibility of addressing Arctic issues related to tourist operators and their capacity to tackle the increasing impact of climate change by altering the basic foundation of visitor expectations in Svalbard. Furthermore, the responsibility of researchers and tourist operators to explain and make clear the impacts of climate change on Svalbard is often present in finding good examples and models for stories of changes over time in an area that is remote and very different for most people who live south of the Arctic Circle. The latter is of course related to the responsibility that tourists have, when seeking out the remote and logistically challenging areas of the far north, to respect and understand the terms and conditions for travels in the fragile Arctic landscapes. These are all issues somewhat related to the ongoing research project Extended Rephotography: Immersive Representations of Climate Change. This project is based in Magdalenefjorden and investigates the possibilities of new technologies for new ways of telling related to the impacts of climate change on the Svalbard landscape. Since we started our project of monitoring and documenting North West Spitsbergen National Park in 2011, our focus area has continuously and increasingly changed. All of the glaciers on the northwestern coasts of Svalbard are melting and losing their appearance that made the landscape so special to early travellers (Martens, 1675; Phipps, 1774; Beechey, 1843; Strindberg, 1897). In some cases, land becomes more accessible and this might open up new perspectives on the views. In other cases, areas known for their beauty in the interaction between ice, rock and mountains lose that colourful appeal offered by glaciers (see Figure 6.4). Communication and applications of immersive visual technologies are key aspects of this project. The work is a collaboration between the Norwegian Polar Institute, the University of Tromsø, Visual Arena Lindholmen Gothenburg, Stockholm University and the University of Gothenburg. The institutions in Tromsø are connected to Polaria, an Arctic experience centre with which we collaborate to present high-end stereo films from fieldwork, telling the stories of the changing landscape in Svalbard (see Figure 6.5). Tromsø is a gateway to the Arctic and a vast number of tourists pass through this northern town each summer on their way north towards Svalbard. They follow a tradition from centuries of Arctic travel. The Covid-19 pandemic halted tourist operations in Svalbard for the two seasons in 2020 and 2021. What will happen in the future is uncertain, as the lack of clients and optional opportunities to remain in the area has been hard for tourism operators in the islands. Whether or not the effects are temporary, only time will tell. Whether tourism in Arctic Svalbard recovers or not, regulations are needed.

The development of virtual tours in the far north is a way of offering more people a chance to "experience" the Arctic. Through a safe setting, contemporary virtual reality and virtual tours offer a simulated encounter with the Arctic. Several aspects work in favour of this development: less impact on the environment, accessible opportunities to "experience" remote parts of the world, safe journeys into harsh and potentially dangerous environments and useful opportunities to learn about the Arctic prior to possible travels to these destinations. No one going to Svalbard will be able to escape the clear evidence of climate change and its rapid effects on the land. The trim lines in old glacier valleys tell their stories of what once was. This particular example can be enhanced through learning tools such as virtual reality or virtual tours that could be used prior to travels or offered as an onboard expanding experience

Figure 6.4 Gullybreen, Magdalenefjorden. Top: tourists and the glacier, 1926–1931.
Carl Müller & Son. Private collection. Bottom: Gullybukta, 2016.

Photo: Tyrone Martinsson

of Arctic travels. Newly formed land revealed by glacier retreat and thaw-
ing permafrost is changing the very ideas we have of the Arctic as a frozen
land. As mentioned earlier, Svalbard has no Indigenous population and never
has. This makes the archipelago even more unique as an Arctic destination.
Nature in Svalbard is inarguably spectacular. Travels up the west coast will
still grant any visitor stunning views of rugged mountains and a rough and
wild landscape, with glaciers covering valleys and mountain ridges. Those
who look more carefully, though, will see the evidence of a changing land. If
we provide the opportunity to make comparisons through old photographs,
the story changes focus. What might look like an undisturbed wilderness is in
fact dramatically affected by a warming climate.

Figure 6.5 Erik Mannerfelt operating a drone in Svalbard, 2016.
Photo: Tyrone Martinsson

The latest research shows that the Arctic is warming four times faster than the rest of the world (Voosen, 2021). How this changing of the Arctic will affect tourists in the future is difficult to predict. Svalbard is a remote and wild place with or without ice. However, one of the most popular and sought-after sights of the Arctic landscape is the polar bear. The changing conditions, with less sea ice, fewer glaciers and warmer summers, is dramatically changing the bears' natural habitat. They are dependent on the marine environment with seals and frozen hunting and mating grounds. They will have increasingly more difficulties finding food; for a while, they will be able to retreat farther northeast, but the prospects for their future are grim. The same fate is awaiting the walrus, the Arctic fox and some of the birds nesting in Svalbard during the Arctic summers. All of these animals have historically been important to the tourist industry, particularly the polar bear. Perhaps future Svalbard travels will include the possibility to experience what was once there through virtual tours or even augmented reality from the ships or during encounters with the land. Future visitors might enter the northern landscapes, perhaps for dramatic hikes, which might become available without the need for guides carrying rifles for bear protection. On-site virtual visual experiences would offer a stunning way to understand the impact of climate change. That possibility is already technically available to be explored by tour operators. New technologies and their extended ways of telling offer the capacity to mix real-life experiences with enhanced virtual visions, increasing the tools for transformative learning concerning climate change. This could aid future tourists from modern industrialized societies in understanding of our connection to nature. In such a scenario, a remote place like Svalbard might be one of the places to go, escaping the crowded cities of southern latitudes and connecting to a past that hopefully shows a path to the future by reminding us of a lost past that might one day be healed and make the north cold again.

References

Banerjee, S. (2017). Long environmentalism – After the listening session. In S. Monani & J. Adamson (Eds.), *Ecocriticism and Indigenous Studies – Conversations from Earth to Cosmos* (pp. 62–81). London: Routledge.

Barker, R. (1819). *Description of a View of the North Coast of Spitzbergen, Now Exhibiting in the Large Rotunda of Henry Aston Barker's Panorama, Leicester-Square; Painted from Drawings taken by Lieut. Beechey who Accompanied the Polar Expedition in 1818 and Liberally Presented Them to the Proprietor*. London: James and Charles Adlard.

Barr, W. (2019). *John Rae, Arctic Explorer, The Unfinished Autobiography*. Edmonton: University of Alberta Press.

Beechey, W. (1843). *A Voyage Of Discovery Towards The North Pole, Performed In His Majesty's Ships Dorothea And Trent, Under The Command Of Captain David Buchan, R.N.; 1818; To Which Is Added, A Summary Of All The Early Attempts To Reach The Pacific By Way Of The Pole. By Captain F.W. Beechey, R.N., F.R.S. One Of The Lieutenants Of The Expedition*. Cambridge: Richard Bentley.

Beke, C. T. (1853). *The three voyages of William Barents to the Arctic regions (1594, 1595, and 1596)*. London: The Hakluyt Society.

Broke, P. (1807). *Magdalena Bay. Spitsbergen*. Taunton: Hydrographic Office.

Capelotti, P. (2011). Review of *Greetings from Spitsbergen: Tourists at the eternal ice, 1827–1914*, by John T. Reilly. *Polar Research*, 30, 5912. https://doi.org/10.3402/polar.v30i0.5912.

Conway, W. M. (1906). *No Man's Land: A History of Spitsbergen from its Discovery in 1596 to the Beginning of the Scientific Exploration of the Country*. Cambridge: Cambridge University Press.

Cruikshank, J. (2005). *Do Glaciers Listen? – Local Knowledge, Colonial Encounters, & Social Imagination*. Vancouver: UBC Press.

Davidson, P. (2005). *The Idea of North*. London: Reaktion Books.

Dowie, M. (2017). *The Haida Gwaii Lesson – A Strategic Playbook for Indigenous Sovereignty*. Oakland: Inkshares.

Gernsheim, H. (1988). *The Rise of Photography 1850–1880: The Age of Collodion*. London: Thames & Hudson.

Hauan, M. A. (2021). *Personal communication*.

Holmes, O. W. (1859, June). The stereoscope and the stereograph. *The Atlantic*.

Lausberg, C. (1913). *Das Nordland.* Leipzig: Klinkhardt & Bierman.

Loomis, C. C. (1977). The Arctic sublime. In U. C. Knoepflmacher & G. B. Tennyson (Eds.), *Nature and the Victorian Imagination* (pp. 95–112). Berkeley, CA: University of California Press.

Martens, F. (1675). *Spitzbergische oder Groenlandische Reise Beschreibung, gethan im Jahr 1671. Aus eigner Erfahrunge beschrieben, die dazu erforderte Figuren nach dem Leben selbst abgerissen, (so hierbey in Kupffer zu sehen) und jetzo durch den Druck mitgetheilet.* Ratingen: Gottfired Schultze.

Martinsson, T. (2015). *Arctic Views: Passages in Time.* Stockholm: Art and Theory Publishing.

Martinsson, T. (2019). The arctic regions – visual stories from a changing north. *PhotoResearcher*, 31, 242–257.

Martinsson, T. (2021). Repeat photography and archives: A humanities-based dialogue with the history of ice in Svalbard. In S. Acadia & M. Fjellestad (Eds.), *Library and Information Studies for Arctic Social Sciences and Humanities* (pp. 199–226). New York: Routledge.

Norwegian Environmental Agency (2021, September 3). *Proposed changes to the regulations in Svalbard.* www.environmentagency.no/news/2021/proposed-changes-to-the-environmental-regulations-in-svalbard

Norwegian Polar Institute (2003). *The Place Names of Svalbard.* Tromsø: Norwegian Polar Institute.

Phipps, C. J. (1774). *A Voyage Towards the North Pole, Undertaken by His Majesty's Command 1773.* Oxford: J. Nourse.

Potter, R. (2007). *Arctic Spectacles: The Frozen North on Visual Culture, 1818–1875.* Seattle, WA: University of Washington Press.

Purchas, S. (1625). *Purchas His Pilgrimes: Contayning a History of the World in Sea Voyages and Lande Travells by Englishmen and Others* (vol. XIV). London: James MacLehose and Sons.

Strindberg, N. (1897). *Karta öfver Amsterdamön med omgifningar.* London: Stockholm.

University of Gothenburg (n.d.). Extended Rephotography: immersive visualization of climate change. https://www.gu.se/en/research/extended-rephotography-immersive-visualization-of-climate-change

Voosen, P. (2021, December 14). The Arctic is warming four times faster than the rest of the world. *Science.org.* https://doi.org/10.1126/science.acz9830.

Wheatstone, C. (1838). Contributions to the physiology of vision. Part the first. On some remarkable, and hitherto unobserved, phenomena of binocular vision. *Philosophical transactions of the Royal Society of London*, 128, 371–394. http://doi.org/10.1098/rstl.1838.0019

Wieder, F. C. (1919). *The Dutch Discovery and Mapping of Spitsbergen (1596–1829).* Amsterdam: Royal Dutch Geograph. Soc.

Wråkberg, U. (1999). *Vetenskapens vikingatåg. Perspektiv på svensk polarforskning 1860–1930.* Uppsala: Uppsala Universitet.

7 Citizen science as a tourist attraction

An active learning tourist experience

Anna Axelsson and Andreas Skriver Hansen

More active and inclusive tourist experiences are increasingly receiving attention within the tourist industry (Mathis et al., 2016). For this reason, there has been considerable focus among tourism operators on specializing in different kinds of active and engaging tourist experiences as a way of standing out and catering to a broad tourist spectrum by offering unique and specialized tourist experiences (Novelli, 2018). As emphasized in chapter 1, part of this trend coincides with a parallel trend wherein tourist expectations have changed towards demanding more out of their experiences, including new learning experiences and outcomes, with a focus on participating in learning processes for the attainment of new knowledge while travelling (Falk et al., 2011). This development and phenomenon we refer to as "learning tourist experiences," which concerns tourism experiences where learning is a central part of or the main focus in the experience.

In learning tourist experiences, tourists may take either a passive or an active role (as discussed in chapter 4), depending on the content of the learning experience. Examples of more passive learning experiences include visits to museums, aquariums and visitor centres, or participating in guided tours where learning outcomes are the results of more passively absorbed information from the experience (Zhang et al., 2018). Active learning tourist experiences (ALTEs), on the other hand, involve tourists assuming a more active learning role in the co-creation of their activities and thus their experiences. Examples of this are typically seen in volunteer tourism or ecotourism, where tourists take an active part and wherein learning and knowledge are often important outcomes (Tomazos & Butler, 2009; Phillips et al., 2019). The uniqueness of ALTE is therefore its place at the intersection between co-creation and learning.

A relatively unexplored branch of ALTE is the potential to integrate citizen science (CS) in order to facilitate learning in the tourist experience. In short, CS can be described as data or knowledge contributions by non-professionals (i.e. citizens) to work by professionals (i.e. experts) (Haklay

DOI: 10.4324/9781003293316-7

et al., 2021). Typically, CS in tourism involves data production, where tourists contribute data for research or management purposes as part of their stay (Schaffer & Tham, 2020). The process may, however, go beyond mere data collection and include important learning aspects, where being part of the experience leads to new learning (Sandiford, 2021). From this perspective, CS becomes an attraction in itself by becoming an experience and knowledge enhancer, with tourists becoming active collaborators and contributors.

The aim of this chapter is to explore and highlight this perspective. This work includes further examination of ALTE as a way of coupling CS with tourism experiences. The empirical basis of the work, and the main focus and contribution in the chapter, is two Swedish case studies presenting new ideas and discussions of the potentials of CS as a tourist attraction. The following questions are raised:

1   How has CS been used in tourism?
2   How can combining CS and the tourist experience be achieved to create an attraction?
3   What are the requirements, challenges and opportunities in combining CS and the tourist experience?

The first question is answered in the following section, which provides the theoretical foundations of ALTE and examples of the use of CS in tourism. The second question is answered by introducing the two case studies and exploring how CS as a tourist experience can become a tourist attraction. Finally, the third question is answered through reflections on the findings towards the end of the chapter.

Citizen science in tourism

Active learning tourism experience and citizen science

ALTE is our own conceptual construction, although it has a strong foundation in experience-based learning forms with a focus on tourists as active co-producers of their own experience outcomes through active engagement (Larsen & Meged, 2013). The emphasis is on "active," as it involves placing the experience outcomes in the hands of the tourists themselves. The concept draws content from many related tourism fields where learning, educational and experiential dimensions are integrated into the tourist experience. Examples include ecotourism (e.g. Stronza et al., 2019), volunteer tourism (e.g. Sandiford, 2021), science tourism (e.g. Bourlon & Torres, 2016), research tourism (e.g. Wood, 2010) and educational tourism (e.g.

Tomasi et al., 2020). To explore the concept in more detail, it is first broken down to its two core parts: the *tourist experience* and *active learning*.

In terms of the tourist experience, the trend that tourists are increasingly demanding more and new kinds of content from their travels rather than solely enjoyment and relaxation aligns with a shift towards an experience-based economy, where consumers expect an added layer of experience along with their consumption of services and products (Pine & Gilmore, 1998). Drawing from this, Oh et al. (2007) suggest four dimensions of experience that are relevant within the tourism sector: aesthetics, education, entertainment and escapism, with a combination of these providing the optimal experience. Falk et al. (2012) build on the educational aspect to argue that the intersection between tourism and learning has become an essential component in the tourist experience. In addition to meeting the increasing demand for travels with meaningful content, Falk et al. assert that this junction can serve society as well as the planet through personal development, including new commitments to and understandings of the world that is experienced.

Active learning in tourism, specifically, can take on many forms. In this chapter, however, the focus is only on active learning tourist experiences in relation to CS, which we use as a way to describe all CS uses in tourism. A definition of CS has been offered, but it is too simplistic, as it does not consider the degree of tourist involvement during the activity. For example, Sauermann et al. (2020) split CS into two rough perspectives: a production perspective, where citizens mainly contribute data, and a democratized perspective, where citizens help construct and facilitate research questions, thus going beyond mere data collection (simple CS) to active learning processes (advanced CS). This is in line with Kasperowski and Kullenberg (2018), who rather view the process as a continuum, moving from simpler to more advanced CS, depending on the process and degree of involvement required from the citizen. Specifically, they emphasize that CS can refer to engagement, where societal development is the prominent focus, rather than its contribution to research. This aspect can be realized through dialogue initiated by actors such as NGOs as well as through the active involvement of civil society in co-creation processes, aimed at achieving political and/or societal agendas. We also view the use of CS in tourism as a continuum rather than as split between the two perspectives. The main point is the learning aspect, where the focus is as much on how the CS experience affects the citizen as it is on how CS assists the experts (Dillon et al., 2016).

Examples

There are numerous different examples of active learning through CS in tourism. To set the scene, Schaffer and Tham (2020) in a recent literature study identified more than 5,700 papers using the words "citizen science" and "tourist." Upon further scrutiny, however, we found that the number of direct examples of CS use is significantly lower and mostly branches off into known tourism subcategories, such as volunteer tourism, ecotourism or educational tourism, where involvement and learning activities are often a part of the experience. For this reason, there is a blurred line between CS in tourist activities and experiences in these more specialized tourism categories. To maintain the focus, we have included only studies where the coupling of CS and tourism is developed beyond mere mention.

By far the largest number of studies focus on environmentally themed projects, where tourists assist in a variety of works on a voluntary or paid basis. Typical examples include tourists involved in monitoring ecological or biological qualities, such as species or resource monitoring, where data collection is merged with active learning experiences that result in knowledge about local ecosystems as well as management and conservation efforts (e.g. Branchini et al., 2015; Ghilardi-Lopes, 2015; Chase & Levine, 2016; Currie et al., 2018; Hermoso et al., 2020). There are also quite a number of studies focusing on documenting the more negative side of human uses of natural resources, often including various impacts on or damage to the physical environment, such as litter, debris and other pollution in nature, or more complex challenges, such as invasive species introduced by human activity. Again, the experience involves a mix of data collection and active learning with an emphasis on understanding the reasons behind and outcomes of the observed problems, and their potential solutions (e.g. Hidalgo-Ruz & Thiel, 2013; Martin, 2013; Bergmann et al., 2017; Nelms et al., 2017; Honorato-Zimmer et al., 2019).

Other, smaller study topics include work on environmental or community conservation in different forms where tourists, through CS initiatives, actively assist local managers in conservation work. Data collection such as that previously described is one example. Another involves direct participation in community development projects with a focus on discussing management and conservation strategies for the resources and communities that tourism depends on. Through these co-creation processes, tourists learn not only about ecosystems and communities but also about community management and governance systems (e.g. Cigliano et al., 2015; dos Santos & Bessa, 2019; Hermoso et al., 2020). Another thread of topics concerns studies of environmental change where tourists, through CS, assist in documenting traces of environmental changes in different settings, e.g. the Arctic or the Great Barrier Reef, where climate impacts and challenges are very real. The learning part involves understanding the reasons for the changes and their environmental and social impacts as well as discussing efforts to counter the negative effects of the development (e.g. de la Barre et al., 2016; Farmer et al., 2016; Gouraguine et al., 2019; Taylor et al., 2020).

Across these studies, there is a consensus that the active involvement of tourists in various scientific, management or NGO-based activities can result in valuable learning outcomes, and that CS is a good means of facilitating such a process. Furthermore, although not stated explicitly in all texts, the CS aspect of the experience is emphasized as contributory in attracting tourists to the place and the experience. In particular, there is an emphasis on how the learning aspect of the experiences may provide opportunities for challenging oneself, acquiring new skills and personal growth, as well as expanding scientific agency and literacy (Sauermann et al., 2020; Schaffer & Tham, 2020).

To further explore how CS as a tourist experience can become a tourist attraction, two case studies are now introduced.

Case study area and methods

The two cases include examples of active learning tourist experiences that connect or can potentially be connected to citizen science. In the first case, the CS aspect concerns participants photographing and reflecting on their own recreational experiences in Kosterhavet National Park. The second case involves an aspect of CS where actors responsible for beach cleaning activities, as well as local municipality representatives, reflect on the potential of using marine litter as a theme to connect CS with tourism. Geographically, both case studies are based on the west coast of Sweden – a popular and important area for both domestic and international tourism (Hansen, 2016). It was therefore considered relevant in answering the second question of the chapter, about how to create an attraction by combining CS and the tourist experience. For an overview of the area, please see the map (Figure 2.1) in chapter 2.

The first case concerns a published paper documenting and analyzing positive and negative recreational experiences in the Kosterhavet National Park (see Hansen, 2016). Kosterhavet is known for its many unique ecological and cultural experience qualities, that is, for experiences with a high ecological or cultural value. However, currently not much is known about important experience qualities in the park, which is a challenge for park management efforts and marketing strategies in the area. Understanding the visitor experience is therefore important for the development of the park and local area. Furthermore, from a research perspective, there is a need to develop methods that allow for a better understanding of the tourism experience (Hansen, 2016). In response to this situation, a combined research and management investigation was launched with a focus on collecting relevant information about the topic and exploring methods to achieve it. For this to work best, it was decided to use a citizen science approach involving visitors actively contributing to data collection (with pictures) and sharing lived experiences (interviews).

Specifically, a methodological approach called "visitor-produced pictures" was used to collect pictures from park visitors. The pictures were to include positive and negative experiences as expressed by the visitors themselves. This was done in order to document and better understand content and variations across experience qualities, as well as preferences among visitors. The method has been described in detail in Hansen (2016).

The second case looks more broadly at the potential of merging CS with local tourism, using marine litter as a theme, as this is both a concrete and well-known subject where CS has the potential to aid with tasks such as mapping distribution, transport or the interaction of litter with marine biota (Hidalgo-Ruz & Thiel, 2015). Moreover, the Swedish west coast is one of the most severely exposed to marine litter in Europe, which further strengthens the relevance of the topic (Bråte et al., 2017). Despite not explicitly working with CS, three local actors arranging beach cleaning activities along the coast were interviewed about the potential of CS as a way to increase attention to the local environment and community. Furthermore, the potential of merging a concept of marine litter and CS with tourism was discussed with a local tourist actor and a municipality representative. They both operate in Strömstad, which is a town that to a large extent depends on maintaining healthy environmental conditions to keep its tourist industry intact. The original report was produced through an explorative process that reveals various perspectives. For a detailed method description, see the full study in Axelsson (2021).

Documenting visitor experiences

Experience qualities in Kosterhavet

Over the course of the summer season of 2014, 41 individuals spanning the most popular recreational groups found in the national park participated in the study: campers, day visitors, kayakers, boaters, second-home owners and locals. This resulted in more than 550 pictures that were subsequently discussed and analyzed together with the participants during individual interviews. The output provided insights into six experience quality categories:

- *natural environments* (Figure 7.1): experiences of various natural elements showing the diversity of the natural environment in the park
- *social situations* (Figure 7.2): experiences featuring social bonding and closeness with friends and family
- *cultural environments* (Figure 7.3): experiences related to the unique cultural environment found in and around Kosterhavet
- *recreational activities* (Figure 7.4): experiences of recreational activities, closely tied to important motivational factors

Figure 7.1 Natural environments.

Source: Author's photo

- *emotional reactions* (Figure 7.5): experiences involving special feelings or sensory output related to the coast or the sea
- *disturbing factors* (Figure 7.6): experiences of disturbances affecting the stay, such as noise, crowding, litter or dogs off leash

The results of the picture documentation and the detailed narratives led to reflections on four outcomes in particular. First, it provided detailed insights into what might constitute important experience qualities, thus helping to build a larger theoretical understanding and framework on the topic. Second, the results proved useful in park management as the detailed information allowed for more informed decision-making and strategic planning regarding safeguarding the experience qualities identified. Third, the study led to increased visitor satisfaction as the participants felt that their contribution had helped shape the planning of the park, essentially becoming an example of visitor democracy and empowerment. Fourth, and most interesting for the coupling of CS and learning, the process of discussing the content in their own pictures led participants to explore their own recreational preferences and likes, or to find new aspects of their stay that they had not noticed before.

Figure 7.2 Social situations.
Source: Author's photo

Specifically, the pictures worked as catalysts to enable them to reflect more deeply about their recreational activities and to open up memories and experiences that the participants would not have thought of otherwise.

Furthermore, the task of taking pictures was often done not alone but together with accompanying travellers, such as friends, family members or partners. This led to discussions among the participants and their travel companions, allowing them to learn more about their experiences together and what qualities drew them to the park. As a result, the participants learnt more about themselves, particularly about their priorities for experiences during their stay in Kosterhavet and how these connect to their travel practices and the settings wherein these take place. These quotes from the participants capture the essence of these learning dimensions, both of the unique Kosterhavet environment but also of themselves in nature:

> Every time I see a flower or a bird or a plant, I try to remember if it's red or black listed, and if you have to protect them or can take them away . . . so you get to learn quite a bit.
>
> (Norwegian kayaker)

Figure 7.3 Cultural environments.
Source: Author's photo

Figure 7.4 Recreational activities.
Source: Author's photo

The learning experience here concerns environmental learning, specifically ecological aspects, such as the recognition of different species and related conservation efforts, which citizens help managers to document in the park.

> It was a very special experience because it was so warm and we had just been taking a swim, but just 5 minutes after, you are already boiling again . . . and then suddenly ending up in this burned landscape in this scorching heat . . . it was like a science fiction movie and we starting wondering which planet we were on . . . but we talked about it and that it might be because they want to maintain the cultural landscape.
>
> (Norwegian sailboater)

This is a learning experience about an important part of the management of the national park: management of the cultural landscape and the practices involved in this work that make the landscape look the way it does.

Figure 7.5 Emotional reactions.
Source: Author's photo

> I found this skeleton, I didn't find it like that, but I had to move it a bit . . . this is the way of nature, somehow. You get close to it if you don't just run by it . . . you learn that things pass on and that things disappear.
>
> (Norwegian camper)

There is an almost poetic touch in this learning experience about life and death, including reflections on the sometimes tough living conditions at sea, an experience and reality that can sometimes be far away from our bustling everyday lives.

> It's [about] a big jellyfish there and about how to explore what is there in the sea . . . it's a bit interesting with the interests of the kids. It starts with playing with nature. They are so used to all their toys back home and now there is so much to explore outside. It is about being allowed to get dirty, to dig up stuff and put your hands in the sand and to walk barefoot on the beach. And not knowing what the things you see are: "What is this? A plant or an animal, or sea grass . . . aha, it's sea grass."
>
> (Swedish day visitor)

Figure 7.6 Disturbing factors.

Source: Author's photo

Through interaction with the environment where you are and which frames your experiences, you learn about it through discovery and curiosity. From a more advanced perspective, this could be an example of ocean literacy taking form.

Tourism attraction potential

In terms of being an attraction, many participants said that it was a fun and fulfilling experience to participate in the study. In fact, contrary to expectations, it did not prove difficult to recruit people to participate, in spite of being in the middle of their vacation time. Many were interested in participating when the purpose of the work was explained to them, and they also encouraged others to participate. As a result, there was almost a movement formed towards the end of the study, where some participants expressed willingness to continue participating on a voluntary basis. A smaller group also said that they felt privileged to be able to help the national park management to improve the conditions of the areas by using their own experiences as a point of interest. Others expressed the fact that they were pleased to be given the chance to document and express feelings of frustration or concern, with a great impact on the quality of their recreational experiences. The result thus became a new approach to participatory resource management built on CS principles.

Above all, many participants expressed the fact that the task became an attraction in itself because of the opportunity for self-discovery and personal reflection. The participants had not signed up to participate in CS work and were not informed about it before arriving in the park, as is a normal procedure within, for instance, volunteer tourism, ecotourism or educational tourism. However, once the opportunity was offered, it was received as a welcome diversion from their normal vacation plans. Based on these reactions, the CS approach was deemed successful in terms of both data delivery and learning outcomes, a combination that ultimately became an attraction, at least during the time that the study was active.

Engaging tourists in voluntary beach cleaning

Citizen science and marine litter

Beach cleaning refers to activities that engage the public on a voluntary basis in the collection of marine litter. Similar to citizen science, it can serve to increase public awareness and, potentially, enhance scientific understanding of the marine litter issue. Beach cleaning events typically involve families, since children can easily be engaged in the activity and can simultaneously gain knowledge about the issue. Interviewees in this case included actors that in a CS-like manner engaged the public in the collection of marine litter. The first actor, Kosterhavets Ekobod, is mainly a restaurant and a cultural scene which organizes public beach cleanings whenever necessary and offers a "beach cleaning coffee" in exchange for a bag of collected litter. In contrast, the work of the second actor, Ocean Crusaders, builds exclusively on beach cleaning through public events, which are managed by employees as well as volunteers. The third actor, Nordic Ocean Watch, is a non-profit organization operating in Denmark, Finland, Norway and Sweden, which, aside from arranging beach cleanings, also focuses on inspiring the public through social media. Additionally, representatives from the tourism sector as well as the municipality of Strömstad were interviewed to investigate the potential of connecting CS with tourism. The tourism representative is the manager of Lagunen, a local camping business, who is interested in establishing a citizen science and marine litter concept, while the municipal representative is an environmental strategist with experience in similar activities.

Profiles, motivation and learning

Concerning the identification of a "typical practitioner" of beach cleaning, all beach cleaning actors mention families with children. Ocean Crusaders and Nordic Ocean Watch also observe that more women than men participate. Additionally, Kosterhavets Ekobod claims that local inhabitants are more represented than tourists are. As such, it appears challenging to identify a common profile. However, Nordic Ocean Watch describes how the organization's activities on Instagram and other social media channels has attracted young adults specifically: "A problem, I think, with many charities is that they have not dared to choose a target group. You try talking to everyone, and then in the end you do not know who you are talking to." This indicates that it is possible to target a specific group, which according to them strengthens the potential to attract tourists. Nordic Ocean Watch also describes how the outreach work of the organization has appeared to be easier in smaller towns, where the local municipality is more willing to cooperate.

All actors assert that engaging the public in beach cleaning on a voluntary basis is not challenging. Rather, it is a popular activity that requires relatively simple elements to generate fascination and interest, and often solely the visibility of the organization is enough. According to Kosterhavets Ekobod, a signboard on the way down to the beach advertising the "beach cleaning coffee" can be enough to compel people to engage in litter collections. Nordic Ocean Watch uses a container within which the collected litter is exhibited. The actors describe how the contents of the container are associated with an underwater museum and say that the feedback from visitors has indicated that it is an attraction. The importance of visibility also became evident to Ocean Crusaders, who describe how the very presence of the organization at beaches creates interest, especially for children passing by their cleaning events; they become curious, and this also engages their parents.

Participatory motivations such as simple snacks are something that all actors use to some degree. However, they do not believe these are the main incentives to engage in beach cleaning. The main reward is rather the feeling of contributing and being part of something meaningful, in response to perceived frustration about increasing reports about marine litter in the media. According to Nordic Ocean Watch, the fact that many beach cleanings are carried out collectively can also connect people socially: "People actually start talking to each other and sometimes I have thought that some came there as friends, but it is rather that they leave as friends."

Since the fundamental challenge regarding marine litter is not solved simply by cleaning beaches, all actors underline the importance of emphasizing learning aspects in relation to the activity. Ocean Crusaders, for example, describe how they use collected rubber boots and other relatable debris to inspire not only participation, but also learning about consequences for the marine environment. Showing old products, such as food packaging dating back to the 1990s, is another way of illustrating how long it takes for debris to break down. According to Nordic Ocean Watch, combining the activity with elements of learning is important in order to "see what kind of litter it is, why it ended up here, how do we solve the problem so that it does not end up here." However, the importance of not overwhelming and not shaming people is also underlined. One example of educating without doing this is by encouraging people to choose reusable products, instead of blaming their usage of disposables.

Tourism attraction potential

The representative from Lagunen is positive about a concept combining CS and marine litter to attract tourists. Since a few years back, an important target group for the company is visitors who value the local natural environment. The representative says that part of their mission is to advocate for smaller ecological footprints among their guests: "There I think we also find the person, the guest who can contribute to CS." Aside from the considerable need for beach cleaning in the local area, the primary value of such a concept would be to enlighten visitors about the issue and thus influence their littering behaviour.

Moreover, incorporating CS within tourism in Strömstad could be a way of building more flexibility and innovation into the industry, while also enhancing the environmental reputation and recognition of the town. Specifically, Lagunen sees the potential in increased interest and awareness in the municipality regarding an environmentally friendly tourism sector to brand and publicize the town. This is supported by the municipality representative, who reflects that beach cleaning is something that is promoted in the town through events or pick-up boxes containing bags, gloves and other essential materials. There are four spots where these can be picked up, including the tourist office, which needs to be resupplied continuously. They also organize preparatory classes for schools as a basis for students to be able to go out and clean, which is a popular activity. The representative emphasizes that "this is the type of area that engages and people want to be involved."

The case illustrates that engaging citizens in beach cleaning activities can be done without concrete rewards or incentives, since the main participatory motivation is often to contribute something meaningful, which essentially becomes an attraction in itself. Learning elements can be specifically incorporated into the activity through simple methods such as visually illustrating the marine litter issue. The case thus indicates a strong potential for merging CS and tourism, as well as willingness to do so on the part of the local tourist industry and the municipality.

Discussion

Citizen science as an attraction

The aim of this chapter was to explore and highlight the potential of citizen science in turning tourists into active collaborators and contributors of experience and knowledge. The two case studies illustrate ideas and discussions about how CS and the tourist experience can be combined through active learning tourist experiences. Specifically, the use of CS shows potential in producing more advanced and fulfilling active learning tourist experiences that can become attractions if they are organized in a way that allows for personal learning opportunities. Common threads in the two examples that emphasize the attractiveness of the CS activity include:

- *active involvement*: the focus is on citizens as active co-producers of their own experiences through active engagement, including experiences of assisting researchers in their work (Larsen & Meged, 2013)
- *enhancement of experience value*: this point goes back to Dillon et al. (2016), who emphasize that the learning aspect is as much about how CS enhances the experience, affecting the citizen, as it is about how CS assists the experts
- *understandable and relatable focus*: this applies to both environmental and community conservation projects where tourists connect with what is observed and done in the field through CS initiatives (Taylor et al., 2020)
- *personal learning/growth*: this builds on the educational aspect emphasized by Falk et al. (2012), who argue that the intersection between tourism and learning has become an important part of the tourist experience

In short, the use of CS in the two examples fulfils the demand for more individualized and engaging tourist experiences, as emphasized earlier. It does so by introducing new learning experiences and outcomes, with a focus on participating in learning processes for the attainment of new knowledge and understanding while travelling. For many, this includes a sense of empowerment and stewardship gained through the work performed, while the experience also offers a good way for local stakeholders and visitors to meet and actively work together to create positive change. The result is a tourism experience with a specific focus on learning about and reflecting on the local context, much like ecotourism or volunteer tourism experiences, but requiring short-term commitment and thus more accessible to people. Furthermore, it confirms the close link to active learning forms in tourism.

Requirements, challenges and opportunities

Both cases illustrate how elements of learning and reflection can be incorporated into daily activities through quite simple methods, such as encouraging photo documentation or managing marine litter. In relation to the third question of the chapter, we have also identified some requirements, challenges and opportunities connected to such activities.

Regarding requirements, one essential key to being successful with CS in tourism and to achieving engagement among tourists is the use of simple methods. It is preferable for these to be easily integrated into a perhaps already established scheme of activities, where participation does not counteract the initial visions of the trip and is not perceived as too demanding (Schaffer & Tham, 2020). This includes clear activity goals and educated instructors who are consistently present and engaged throughout the work, for instance by analyzing experiences and results together with participants. Something that can further spur the motivation of continued participation is if the results of the project are communicated and accessible, as in the example of the container with collected litter on display. This can aid the feeling of purpose through contribution (Taylor et al., 2020). In this case, and following existing findings in the literature, the ability to examine personal benefits is important, since the urge to make a concrete effort for the local destination, environment or community is often the main participatory motivation, as illustrated in both cases. Moreover, continuity and planning are crucial in order to anchor and profile the experience as a local phenomenon and attraction, as emphasized by the local stakeholders in Kosterhavet.

Some of the challenges we foresee in terms of combining CS and tourism concern the more practical aspects. Examples include the process of establishing the experience as being time consuming and costly, both in terms of preparing and executing it. Furthermore, scientists, as well as managers and others invested in tourism, may not have the necessary skills and competences to work with CS, so specialist education may be needed. This was especially the case in the picture study, where the managers relied on the researchers to undertake the study, while realizing their own deficits in terms of more qualitative visitor approaches. Another challenge is that tourist motivations and engagement levels vary and shift frequently, depending on experience trends and demands. In other words, what is popular one year may not be so popular the following year. For instance, the initiatives by Kosterhavets Ekobod, Ocean Crusaders and Nordic Ocean Watch work well now because of an increased focus on environmental responsibility in today's society, but such trends may change in a decade or two. Consequently, working towards making CS an attraction in tourism, and keeping a level of interest, requires a high degree of outlook and adaptation from an organizational point of view. Finally, a third challenge is to reach and motivate tourists other than the most enthusiastic ones (typically eco-volunteer tourists). In this case, better and broader profiling may be needed, meaning that CS activities must be made accessible and understandable across a wide variety of tourist segments. In this, we see the potential of integrating CS into the tourist experience as a positive factor and as a quality stamp for tourism overall.

Concerning opportunities, one of the more important outcomes of making CS a tourist attraction is the potential benefits of such an experience. For example, both case studies emphasize how engagement in local contexts and self-reflection can strengthen or lead to increased environmental and community awareness. The result is a tourist experience with transformative learning qualities that may produce enlightened citizens and inspire individual and collective action. If this can be achieved, it may lead to accomplishing larger societal and environmental goals, including the UN 2030 Agenda (Fritz et al., 2019). Furthermore, it may be a way to take a symbolic step away from more passive tourism forms and may also be a countermeasure to growing environmental and social concerns surrounding the fast-growing tourist industry of today. In fact, it could be argued that the process of making CS a tourist attraction makes tourist activities relevant and present with the ability to inspire environmental and social responsibility. Ultimately, the product may therefore give rise to new thinking within the tourist industry itself, as new demands based on these values are likely to increase in the future (Oh et al., 2007). Additionally, not just the tourist industry, but also other CS organizers, including researchers, can find inspiration. For instance, the use of CS as a part of the tourist experience may provide tourism researchers with new perspectives and options to study the tourist experience more thoroughly. Furthermore, CS organizers are often concerned with attracting volunteers, and therefore share an interest in understanding how learning experiences through CS can become attractive in and of themselves.

This chapter concludes that citizen science can be made into a strong tourist experience enhancer that has the potential to become a tourist attraction. At the same time, we acknowledge that our two case studies merely provide indications and suggestions, and that the two examples are not enough to make a strong argument for CS use in tourism just yet. To succeed with this, we propose that the topic should be explored further by receiving more research attention, including new case studies for comparison and further theoretical development in relation to established learning approaches such as active and experience-based learning.

110   *Anna Axelsson and Andreas Skriver Hansen*

References

Axelsson, A. (2021). *Medborgarforskning som turistattraktion – En kartläggning av medborgarforskning och dess potential inom maritim turism* (CFT-Rapport 2021:01). https://gupea.ub.gu.se/handle/2077/68359

Bergmann, M., Lutz, B., Tekman, M. B., & Gutow, L. (2017). Citizen scientists reveal: Marine litter pollutes Arctic beaches and affects wild life. *Marine Pollution Bulletin*, 125(1–2), 535–540. https://doi.org/10.1016/j.marpolbul.2017.09.055

Bourlon, F., & Torres, R. (2016). *Scientific Tourism, A Tool for Tourism Development in Patagonia*. PACTE, Université Grenoble Alpes & CIEP. https://labex-item.hypotheses.org/177

Branchini, S., Meschini, M., Covi, C., Piccinetti, C., Zaccanti, F., & Goffredo, S. (2015). Participating in a citizen science monitoring program: Implications for environmental education. *PLoS ONE*, 10(7). https://doi.org/10.1371/journal.pone.0131812

Bråte, I. L., Bastian, H., Thomas, K., Eidsvoll, D., Halsband, C., Carney Almroth, B., & Lusher, A. (2017). *Micro- and Macro-plastics in Marine Species from Nordic Waters* (TemaNord 2017: 549). Nordic Council of Ministers. https://norden.diva-portal.org/smash/get/diva2:1141513/FULLTEXT02.pdf

Chase, S. K., & Levine, A. (2016). A framework for evaluating and designing citizen science programs for natural resources monitoring. *Conservation Biology*, 30(3), 456–466. https://doi.org/10.1111/cobi.12697

Cigliano, J., Meyer, R., Ballard, H., Freitag, A., Phillips, T., & Wasser, A. (2015). Making marine and coastal citizen science matter. *Ocean & Coastal Management*, 115, 77–87. https://doi.org/10.1016/j.ocecoaman.2015.06.012

Currie, J. J., Stack, S. H., & Kaufman, G. D. (2018). Conservation and education through ecotourism: Using citizen science to monitor cetaceans in the four-island region of Maui, Hawaii. *Tourism in Marine Environments*, 13, 65–71. https://doi.org/10.3727/154427318X15270394903273

de la Barre, S., Maher, P. T., Dawson, J., Hillmer-Pegram, K. C., Huijbens, E. H., Lamers, M., Liggett, D., Müller, D. K., Pashkevich, A., & Stewart, E. J. (2016). Tourism and Arctic observation systems: Exploring the relationships. *Polar Research*, 35. 10.3402/polar.v35.24980

Dillon, J., Stevenson, R. B., & Wals, A. E. (2016). Introduction to the special section moving from citizen to civic science to address wicked conservation problems. *Conservation Biology*, 30, 450–455. https://doi.org/10.1111/cobi.12689

dos Santos, P. V., & Bessa, E. (2019). Dolphin conservation can profit from tourism and Citizen science. *Environmental Development*, 32. https://doi.org/10.1016/j.envdev.2019.100467

Falk, J. H., Ballantyne, R. R., Packer, J., & Benckendorff, P. J. (2012). Travel and learning: A neglected tourism research area. *Annals of Tourism Research*, 39, 908–927. https://doi.org/10.1016/j.annals.2011.11.016

Farmer, L., Cowan, A., Hutchings, J. K., & Perovich, D. (2016), Citizen scientists train a thousand eyes on the North Pole. *Eos*, 97. https://doi.org/10.1029/2016EO054989

Fritz, S., See, L., Carlson, T., Haklay, M., Oliver, J.L., Fraisl, D., Mondardini, R., Brocklehust, M., Shanley, L.A., Schade, S., Wehn, U., Abrate, T., Anstee, J., Arnold, S., Billot, M., Campbell, J., Espey, J., Gold, M., Hager, G., He, S.,

Hepburn, L., Hsu, A., Long, D., Masó, J., McCallum, I., Muniafu, M., Moorthy, I., Obersteiner, M., Parker, A.J., Weisspflug, M. & West, S. (2019). Citizen science and the United Nations Sustainable Development Goals. *Nature Sustainability*, 2, 922–930. https://doi.org/10.1038/s41893-019-0390-3

Ghilardi-Lopes, N. (2015). Citizen science combined with environmental education can be a powerful tool for coastal-marine management. *Journal of Coastal Zone Management*, 18, 1–3. https://doi.org/10.4172/2473-3350.1000407

Gouraguine, A., Moranta, J., Ruiz-Frau, A., Hinz, H., Reñones, O., Ferse, S. C., Jompa, J., & Smith, D. J. (2019). Citizen science in data and resource-limited areas: A tool to detect long-term ecosystem changes. *PLoS ONE*, 14. https://doi.org/10.1371/journal.pone.0210007

Haklay, M., Dörler, D., Heigl, F., Manzoni, M., Hecker, S., & Vohland, K. (2021). What is citizen science? The challenges of definition. In K. Vohland, A. Land-Zandstra, L. Ceccaroni, R. Lemmens, J. Perelló, M. Ponti, R. Samson, & K. Wagenknecht (Eds.), *The Science of Citizen Science* (pp. 13–34). New York: Springer. https://doi.org/10.1007/978-3-030-58278-4_2

Hansen, A. S. (2016). Testing visitor produced pictures as a management strategy to study visitor experience qualities – A Swedish marine case study. *Journal of Outdoor Recreation and Tourism*, 14, 52–64. https://doi.org/10.1016/j.jort.2016.05.001

Hermoso, M., Narváez, S., & Thiel, M. (2020). Engaging recreational scuba divers in marine citizen science: Differences according to popularity of the diving area. *Aquatic Conservation-Marine and Freshwater Ecosystems*, 31(2), 441–455. https://doi.org/10.1002/aqc.3466

Hidalgo-Ruz, V., & Thiel, M. (2013). Distribution and abundance of small plastic debris on beaches in the SE Pacific (Chile): A study supported by a citizen science project. *Marine Environmental Research*, 87–88, 12–18. https://doi.org/10.1016/j.marenvres.2013.02.015

Hidalgo-Ruz, V., & Thiel, M. (2015). The contribution of citizen scientists to the monitoring of marine litter. In M. Bergmann, L. Gutow, & M. Klages (Eds.), *Marine Anthropogenic Litter* (pp. 429–447). Cham, Heidelberg, New York, Dordrecht, London: Springer. https://doi.org/10.1007/978-3-319-16510-3_16

Honorato-Zimmer, D., Kruse, K., Knickmeier, K., Weinmann, A., Hinojosa, I. A., & Thiel, M. (2019). Interhemispherical shoreline surveys of anthropogenic marine debris – A binational citizen science project with schoolchildren. *Marine Pollution Bulletin*, 138, 464–473. https://doi.org/10.1016/j.marpolbul.2018.11.048

Kasperowski, D., & Kullenberg, C. (2018). Medborgarforskning och vetenskapens demokratisering – förväntningar, former & förtroende (2018:R3). *Formas*. https://formas.se/analys-och-resultat/publikationer/2018-12-26-medborgarforskning-och-vetenskapens-demokratisering.html

Larsen, J., & Meged, J. W. (2013). Tourists co-producing guided tours. *Scandinavian Journal of Hospitality and Tourism*, 13(2), 88–102. https://doi.org/10.1080/15022250.2013.796227

Martin, J. M. (2013). Marine debris removal: One year of effort by the Georgia sea turtle-center-marine debris initiative. *Marine Pollution Bulletin*, 74(1), 165–169. https://doi.org/10.1016/j.marpolbul.2013.07.009

112   *Anna Axelsson and Andreas Skriver Hansen*

Mathis, E., Kim, H.,Uysal, M., Sirgy, J., & Prebensen, N. (2016). The effect of co-creation experience on outcome variable. *Annals of Tourism Research*, 57, 62–75. https://doi.org/10.1016/j.annals.2015.11.023

Nelms, S. E., Coombes, C., Foster, L. C., Galloway, T. S., Godley, B. J., Lindeque, P. K., & Witt, M. J. (2017). Marine anthropogenic litter on British beaches: A 10-year nationwide assessment using citizen science data. *Science of The Total Environment*, 578, 1399–1409. https://doi.org/10.1016/j.scitotenv.2016.11.137

Novelli, M. (2018). Niche tourism: Past, present and future. In C. Cooper, S. Volo, W. Gartner, & N. Scott (Eds.), *The Sage Handbook of Tourism Management* (pp. 344–359). Los Angeles: Sage Publications.

Oh, H., Fiore, A.-M., & Jeoung, M. (2007). Measuring experience economy concepts: Tourism applications. *Journal of Travel Research*, 46, 119–132. https://doi.org/10.1177/0047287507304039

Phillips, T. B., Ballard, H. L., Lewenstein, B. V., & Bonney, R. (2019). Engagement in science through citizen science: Moving beyond data collection. *Science Education*, 103, 665–690. https://doi.org/10.1002/sce.21501

Pine, J., & Gilmore, J. H. (1998). Welcome to the experience economy. *Harvard Business Review*. https://hbr.org/1998/07/welcome-to-the-experience-economy

Sandiford, P. J. (2021). Volunteer tourists as scientifically aware environmental citizens: Citizen science within an Australian non-governmental organization. *Australasian Journal of Environmental Management*, 28(3), 248–266. https://doi.org/10.1080/14486563.2021.1957031

Sauermann, H., Vohland, K., Antoniou, V., Balázs, B., Göbel, C., Karatzas, K. D., Mooney, P., Perelló, J., Ponti, M., Samson, R., & Winter, S. (2020). Citizen science and sustainability transitions. *Research Policy*, 49. https://doi.org/10.1016/j.respol.2020.103978

Schaffer, V., & Tham, A. (2020). Engaging tourists as citizen scientists in marine tourism. *Tourism Review*, 75(2), 333–346. https://doi.org/10.1108/TR-10-2018-0151

Stronza, A., Carter, A. H., & FitzGerald, L. (2019). Ecotourism for conservation? *Annual Review of Environment and Resources*, 44, 229–253. https://doi.org/10.1146/annurev-environ-101718-033046

Taylor, A. R., Barðadóttir, Þ., Auffret, S., Bombosch, A., Cusick, A. L., Falk, E., & Lynnes, A. (2020). Arctic expedition tourism and citizen science: A vision for the future of polar tourism. *Journal of Tourism Futures*, 6(1), 102–111. http://doi.org/10.1108/JTF-06-2019-0051

Tomasi, S., Paviotti, G., & Cavicchi, A. (2020). Educational tourism and local development: The role of universities. *Sustainability*, 12, 6766. https://doi.org/10.3390/su12176766

Tomazos, K., & Butler, R. (2009). Volunteer tourism: The new ecotourism? *Anatolia*, 20(1), 196–212. https://doi.org/10.1080/13032917.2009.10518904

Wood, P. (2010). *A conceptual exploration of marine research tourism in Australia: A study of the conceptual, supply, and demand nature of marine research tourism in Australia*. Doctoral dissertation. Townsville: James Cook University.

Zhang, H., Chang, P., & Tsai, M. F. (2018). How physical environment impacts visitors' behavior in learning-based tourism – The example of technology museum. *Sustainability*, 10, 3880. https://doi.org/10.3390/su10113880

8 Towards a research agenda on tourism, knowledge and learning

Eva Maria Jernsand, Maria Persson and Erik Lundberg

This book contributes to our understanding of how knowledge and learning in a tourism context can create attractive experiences but can also change people and societies. Based on theories of experience-based and transformational learning, the book provides examples of tourism experiences that engage us and shows how they can form a basis for the creation of new knowledge, change behaviours and change worldviews. Also, from a management perspective, the book provides conceptualizations that may change established communication practices and patterns of collaboration and, in the long run, lead to more sustainable development.

As we reflect on actual experiences, we learn, and we use the experiences in new situations (Kolb, 1984; Lewin, 1946; Piaget, 1952). From an individual and consumer perspective, this results in personal growth as it connects to our interests, previous knowledge and identity (Falk et al., 2012). The more experience we gain, the more adventurous and self-confident we become, and the more we want to develop our skills and find answers to our questions (Savener, 2013). Therefore, experiential and transformational learning is interesting from a sustainable tourism perspective. Visitors may adapt or change behaviours when they return home (Ballantyne et al., 2011) and even change their thoughts, opinions and worldviews (Mezirow, 1990; Reisinger, 2013). Ultimately, as a result of their confrontation with critical moments and immersion in new knowledge when travelling, their awareness increases and could lead to more sustainable development (e.g. increased protection of cultural and natural resources (Han & Hyun, 2017; Persson, 2019).

In this book, the examples include the use of information panels, tour guiding, citizen science, photography and virtual reality, as well as establishments such as museums, research stations and science centres. The biosphere reserve serves as an example of a destination that offers opportunities for learning on a larger scale: the learning destination. In this concluding

DOI: 10.4324/9781003293316-8

chapter, we summarize and synthesize the findings from the book's chapters into four themes: *from passive to active, from analogue to digital, from generic to target group–adapted,* and *from fragmented to inclusive.* These themes reflect transitions –observed transitions (e.g. the digital transition), desirable transitions (linked to research findings and/or normative positions, such as a more sustainable society) or possible transitions (that could further the development of tourism linked to knowledge and learning). Following the themes, we propose ways forward for future research in the field of tourism, knowledge and learning.

From passive to active

Several chapters emphasize that learning is furthered by individualized, engaging and immersive tourist experiences, or in other words more active tourists who co-create experiences or reflect actively upon their lived experiences. Zillinger and Nilsson (chapter 4) define passive learning in a tourism context as people listening to others talking, developing skills by chance or accumulating life experiences over time. In contrast, active learning refers to the search for knowledge, an attempt to master a task, or the pursuit of a valued and abstract knowledge. Organizations, managers and guides can create opportunities for active learning.

But is active tourism a prerequisite for learning? Based on the chapters in this book, learning will probably depend on the provider's communication style, the activity itself and the context of the experience. Lundberg et al. (chapter 3) assume that the professional guide, service provider or researcher as expert can provide opportunities for immersive and highly engaging science tourism experiences. Axelsson and Hansen (chapter 7) dig further into citizen science as a specific type of science tourism, through which easily accessible activities become attractions in and of themselves: tourists' photo documentation and beach cleaning. These are illustrative examples of how active participation can strengthen the learning process.

Although the book provides only a handful of examples of active learning in tourism, this knowledge can form the basis for new methods and practices and further research. Future research should, for instance, elaborate on the conceptual models of science tourism (chapter 3), active and passive learning (chapter 4), TORE (theme, organized, relevant and enjoyable) (chapter 5) and ALTE (active learning tourism experience) (chapter 7). This implies that we need further research that looks into active tourism from both the consumer perspective, linked to, for example, tourists' travel motives (see, e.g., Pearce & Lee, 2005), and the producer perspective, linked to, for example, co-creation, collaboration and the tourism ecosystem (see, e.g., Hsu et al., 2017). Later in this chapter we elaborate on the importance of the latter for the production of learning in tourism.

From analogue to digital

The step into the digital era is discussed in chapters 4, 5, 6 and 7. Digital formats provide novel ways of visualizing, sharing and co-producing knowledge, which could facilitate learning. Today, it is possible to activate, engage and feel connections with and belonging to other participants through digital platforms, creating benefits for everyone involved. With the Covid pandemic, we saw the rise of digital solutions, e.g. the use of digital technologies in museums (see, e.g., Raimo et al., 2021) and the emergence of digital events and festivals (see, e.g., Armbrecht et al., 2021). The crisis forced many tourism actors to take a giant digital leap forward, leading to a significantly increased supply of digital products. One example in this book is platforms offering free guided tours (chapter 4). Of particular interest is the opportunity to learn and experience without travelling, which has enabled us to experience nature and heritage from our homes. An intriguing example is the use of augmented and virtual reality to understand the impacts of climate change in the Arctic (chapter 6).

Although the digital age creates opportunities, it also poses challenges. It is vital to emphasize the threats of digitization, particularly in relation to knowledge mediation and learning. Digital platforms have facilitated the spread of conspiracy theories, false claims and lies that challenge the control of knowledge production that has historically been claimed by institutions such as universities, research centres and government agencies (Oliveira et al., 2022). There is an urgent need for tourism researchers and other actors to address this challenge and how it affects tourist learning and tourist experiences.

From generic to target group–adapted

Is there a place for information panels, human guides and other types of analogue knowledge mediators in this digital era? Of course. It is important to explore the interplay between the digital and the analogue, for example between information panels and virtual guided tours, or how social media furthers physical travel for personal development. This convergence of physical and digital experiences needs more attention in the context of tourism, knowledge and learning. It could draw on existing research that discusses the role of technology as a mediator in tourism experiences (see Urquhart, 2019).

Related to the digital and the analogue and to personal development is the discussion on the adaptation of tourist products and services for different audiences (e.g. older/younger tourists, experienced/inexperienced tourists, tourists with different cultural capital and backgrounds). If we cannot understand and relate to the knowledge that is presented, it does not engage us and does not lead to learning (as discussed in chapter 5). For example, recent research on digital cultural heritage experiences shows that knowledge being made available digitally does not automatically make it more accessible and equitable. Learning is personal and depends on several crucial aspects such as prior knowledge, background and technical competence (Illsley, 2021), which is important to keep in mind in future research on digitization. To offer products and services for different audiences and target groups is equally relevant in analogue settings. At first glance, the target group can simply be interpreted as "the tourist," but different activities and contexts attract different visitors who have differing learning styles, preferences, motives and abilities (see, e.g., Räikkönen et al., 2021). More research is needed on who visits tourism sites focusing on learning experiences and what their prior knowledge and preferences are, so that activities and communication efforts become meaningful for these visitors, and thus deliver learning experiences.

From fragmented to inclusive

In order to create learning experiences, learning organizations and learning destinations, there is a need for close collaborations with stakeholders. This is a reoccurring theme in tourism research as tourism is a very fragmented sector covering various disciplines, authorities and industries (see chapter 3). Residents are both owners of the destination and co-creators of the experience and target groups, and the roles of co-creators and target groups also apply to tourists.

This book does not in any way cover all aspects of collaboration, but it does contribute some examples and conceptualizations. In chapter 2, the reader is introduced to the collaborative process of initiating a UNESCO biosphere reserve. This process builds upon a strong existing collaborative culture in the region, where universities, schools, authorities, businesses and local communities have worked together to develop and communicate knowledge in tourism contexts. In chapter 3, science tourism is conceptualized, presenting universities and research centres as producers not only of knowledge but also of science tourism activities. To varying degrees, they are embedded in both the tourism industry and in science, depending on context. In chapter 7, the tourist is a co-creator in science through the concept of citizen science, while in chapter 4, the essence of guiding is referred to as human interaction. In short, from a broader perspective, tourism may well contribute to learning if we take advantage of colleagues, platforms and networks. It is not only a matter of public-private partnerships, but an overarching perspective of inclusiveness, where it is just as important to build on existing networks as to explore and develop new collaboration opportunities (Hall, 2019). To take a popular term, we may define it as "the tourism ecosystem," a socio-economic system where actors are dependent on each other and on the surrounding physical and digital environment (see Hsu et al., 2017). Further research should focus on knowledge and learning within this tourism ecosystem.

Summary of the research agenda

In this book, we have pointed out the possibilities of tourism learning experiences. Several of the chapters have highlighted that there is a need to develop how such learning experiences are organized. Based on the four themes we have presented, we therefore want to encourage future research that addresses the following questions:

1   *What role does the tourist have in creating active tourist learning experiences, in relation to the provider and other tourists?* We need to better understand how the tourist can be made active in co-creating learning experiences, but also which tourists want to be more active and seek learning and personal development, and to what degree.

2   *What are the positive and negative impacts of the digital transition, in relation to tourism, knowledge and learning?* We need to understand the optimal ways of using digital resources on the part of both providers and consumers to create inclusive learning experiences.

3   *How can providers create inclusive and accessible learning products and services based on tourists' prior knowledge and preferences?* This implies a deeper knowledge about different target groups linked to, for example, culture heritage experiences, science tourism and citizen science experiences.

4   *What is the role of collaboration in providing tourist learning experiences?* The role of collaboration and co-creation is already a well-researched topic in tourism studies, but not as much related to the intersection between tourism, knowledge and learning. Novel stakeholders in the tourism industry, such as different knowledge producers, would need to be included in such studies.

In general, more empirical studies are needed to approach these questions. There is a need to leave the conceptual stage and observe, explore and measure relevant concepts using both qualitative and quantitative methods.

This will generate an even deeper understanding of how tourism can create learning experiences and inform research and practice.

References

Armbrecht, J., Lundberg, E., Pettersson, R., & Zillinger, M. (2021). Swedish sports clubs and events during the Covid 19 pandemic impacts and responses. In V. Ziakas, V. Antchak, & D. Getz (Eds.), *Crisis Management and Recovery for Events: Impacts and Strategies*. Oxford: Goodfellow Publishers. https://doi.org/10.23912/9781911635901-4814

Ballantyne, R., Packer, J., & Sutherland, L. A. (2011). Visitors' memories of wildlife tourism: Implications for the design of powerful interpretive experiences. *Tourism Management*, 32(4), 770–779. https://doi.org/10.1016/j.tourman.2010.06.012

Falk, J. H., Ballantyne, R., Packer, J., & Benckendorff, P. (2012). Travel and learning: A neglected tourism research area. *Annals of Tourism Research*, 39(2), 908–927. https://doi.org/10.1016/j.annals.2011.11.016

Hall, C. M. (2019). Constructing sustainable tourism development: The 2030 agenda and the managerial ecology of sustainable tourism. *Journal of Sustainable Tourism*, 27(7), 1044–1060. https://doi.org/10.1080/09669582.2018.1560456

Han, H., & Hyun, S. S. (2017). Fostering customers' pro-environmental behavior at a museum. *Journal of Sustainable Tourism*, 25(9), 1240–1256. https://doi.org/10.1080/09669582.2016.1259318

Hsu, A. Y. C., King, B., Wang, D., & Buhalis, D. (2017). Entrepreneurship in the contemporary tourism ecosystem: The case of incoming tour operators in Taiwan. In *Information and Communication Technologies in Tourism 2017* (pp. 101–113). Cham: Springer.

Illsley, W. R. (2021). *Assembling the Historic Environment: Heritage in the Digital Making*. Göteborg: Göteborgs Universitet. https://hdl.handle.net/2077/69927

Kolb, D. (1984). *Experiential Learning: Experience as the Source of Learning and Development*. Englewood Cliffs, NJ: Prentice Hall

Lewin, K. (1946). Action research and minority problems. *Journal of Social Issues*, 2(4), 34–46.

Mezirow, J. (1990). How critical reflection triggers transformative learning. *Fostering Critical Reflection in Adulthood*, 1(20), 1–6.

Oliveira, T., Wang, Z., & Xu, J. (2022). Scientific disinformation in times of epistemic crisis: Circulation of conspiracy theories on social media platforms. *Online Media and Global Communication*. https://doi.org/10.1515/omgc-2022-0005

Pearce, P. L., & Lee, U.-I. (2005). Developing the travel career approach to tourist motivation. *Journal of Travel Research*, 43(3), 226–237. https://doi.org/10.1177%2F0047287504272020

Persson, M. (2019). *Science tourism och kunskapsturismens möjligheter*. Delrapport 3 Kunskapsturism. Maritim utveckling i Bohuslän.

Piaget, J. (1952). Jean Piaget. In E. G. Boring, H. Werner, H. S. Langfeld, & R. M. Yerkes (Eds.), *A History of Psychology in Autobiography* (vol. 4, pp. 237–256). Worcester, MA: Clark University Press. https://doi.org/10.1037/11154-011

Räikkönen, J., Grénman, M., Rouhiainen, H., Honkanen, A., & Sääksjärvi. I. E. (2021). Conceptualizing nature-based science tourism: A case study of Seili Island, Finland. *Journal of Sustainable Tourism*. https://doi.org/10.1080/09669 582.2021.1948553

Raimo, N., De Turi, I., Ricciardelli, A., & Vitolla, F. (2021). Digitalization in the cultural industry: Evidence from Italian museums. *International Journal of Entrepreneurial Behavior & Research*. https://doi.org/10.1108/IJEBR-01-2021-0082

Reisinger, Y. (2013). Preface. In Y. Reisinger (Ed.), *Transformational Tourism: Tourist Perspectives* (pp. xii–xiv). Wallingford: CABI

Savener, A. (2013). 11 Finding themselves in San Blas, Panama. In Y. Reisinger (Ed.), *Transformational Tourism: Tourist Perspectives* (pp. 136–148). Wallingford: CABI

Urquhart, E. (2019). Technological mediation in the future of experiential tourism. *Journal of Tourism Futures*, 5(2), 120–126. https://doi.org/10.1108/JTF-04-2019-0033

Index

Note: Page numbers in *italics* indicates figures and page numbers in **bold** indicates tables on the corresponding page.

Printed in the United States
Baker & Taylor Publisher Services

Printed in the United States
by Baker & Taylor Publisher Services